The Making of Crusading Heroes and Villains

Engaging the Crusades is a series of volumes which offer windows into a newly emerging field of historical study: the memory and legacy of the crusades. Together these volumes examine the reasons behind the enduring resonance of the crusades and present the memory of crusading in the modern period as a productive, exciting, and much needed area of investigation.

This new volume explores the ways in which significant crusading figures have been employed as heroes and villains, and by whom. Each chapter analyses a case study relating to a key historical figure including the First Crusader Tancred; 'villains' Reynald of Châtillon and Conrad of Montferrat; the oft-overlooked Queen Melisende of Jerusalem; the entangled memories of Richard 'the Lionheart' and Saladin; and the appropriation of St Louis IX by the British. Through fresh approaches, such as a new translation of the inscriptions on the wreath laid on Saladin's tomb by Kaiser Wilhelm II, this book represents a significant cutting-edge intervention in thinking about memory, crusader medievalism, and the processes of making heroes and villains.

The Making of Crusading Heroes and Villains is the perfect tool for scholars and students of the crusades, and for historians concerned with the development of reputations and memory.

Mike Horswell completed his PhD at Royal Holloway, University of London, and is the author of *The Rise and Fall of British Crusader Medievalism, c. 1825–1945* (2018). He is a Fellow of the Royal Historical Society and is currently researching, teaching, and writing about the memory and use of the crusades in the modern era.

Kristin Skottki is Junior Professor of Medieval History at the University of Bayreuth. She has published on the medieval and modern historiography of the First Crusade, as in her monograph *Christen, Muslime und der Erste Kreuzzug* (2015). Her current research focuses on late medieval piety and medievalism.

ENGAGING THE CRUSADES

THE MEMORY AND LEGACY OF THE CRUSADES

SERIES EDITORS
JONATHAN PHILLIPS AND MIKE HORSWELL

Engaging the Crusades
The Memory and Legacy of Crusading

Engaging the Crusades is a series of volumes which offer initial windows into the ways in which the crusades have been used in the last two centuries; demonstrating that the memory of the crusades is an important and emerging subject. Together these studies suggest that the memory of the crusades, in the modern period, is a productive, exciting, and much needed area of investigation.

Series Editors: Jonathan Phillips and Mike Horswell, Royal Holloway, University of London, UK.

In this series:

Perceptions of the Crusades from the Nineteenth to the Twenty-First Century
Engaging the Crusades, Volume One
Edited by Jonathan Phillips and Mike Horswell

The Crusades in the Modern World
Engaging the Crusades, Volume Two
Edited by Mike Horswell and Akil N. Awan

Controversial Histories – Current Views on the Crusades
Engaging the Crusades, Volume Three
Edited by Felix Hinz and Johannes Meyer-Hamme

The Making of Crusading Heroes and Villains
Engaging the Crusades, Volume Four
Edited by Mike Horswell and Kristin Skottki

For more information about this series, please visit: https://www.routledge.com/Engaging-the-Crusades/book-series/ETC

The Making of Crusading Heroes and Villains

Engaging the Crusades, Volume Four

Edited by Mike Horswell and Kristin Skottki

LONDON AND NEW YORK

First published 2021
by Routledge
2 Park Square, Milton Park, Abingdon, Oxon OX14 4RN

and by Routledge
52 Vanderbilt Avenue, New York, NY 10017

Routledge is an imprint of the Taylor & Francis Group, an informa business

© 2021 selection and editorial matter, Mike Horswell and Kristin Skottki; individual chapters, the contributors

The right of Mike Horswell and Kristin Skottki to be identified as the authors of the editorial material, and of the authors for their individual chapters, has been asserted in accordance with sections 77 and 78 of the Copyright, Designs and Patents Act 1988.

All rights reserved. No part of this book may be reprinted or reproduced or utilised in any form or by any electronic, mechanical, or other means, now known or hereafter invented, including photocopying and recording, or in any information storage or retrieval system, without permission in writing from the publishers.

Trademark notice: Product or corporate names may be trademarks or registered trademarks, and are used only for identification and explanation without intent to infringe.

British Library Cataloguing-in-Publication Data
A catalogue record for this book is available from the British Library

Library of Congress Cataloging-in-Publication Data
Names: Horswell, Mike, editor. | Skottki, Kristin, 1981-editor.
Title: The making of crusading heroes and villains /
edited by Mike Horswell and Kristin Skottki.
Description: New York: Routledge, 2020. |
Series: Engaging the Crusades; vol 4 | Includes bibliographical references and index.
Identifiers: LCCN 2020014172 | ISBN 9780367264444 (v. 4; hardback) | ISBN 9780429293283 (v. 4; ebook)
Subjects: LCSH: Crusades–Biography.
Classification: LCC D156 .M34 2020 | DDC 909.07–dc23
LC record available at https://lccn.loc.gov/2020014172

ISBN: 978-0-367-26444-4 (hbk)
ISBN: 978-0-429-29328-3 (ebk)

Typeset in Times New Roman
by Deanta Global Publishing Services, Chennai, India

Contents

List of figures ix
Acknowledgements x
Abbreviations xi
List of contributors xii

Introduction: making heroes and villains 1
MIKE HORSWELL AND KRISTIN SKOTTKI

1 **'Most Excellent and Brave of Heart': Tancred's making and unmaking in the sources** 7
FRANCESCA PETRIZZO

2 **The memorialisation of Queen Melisende of Jerusalem: from the medieval to the modern** 25
DANIELLE E.A. PARK

3 **Oppressor, martyr, and Hollywood villain: Reynald of Châtillon and the representation of crusading violence** 42
JOHN D. COTTS

4 **'The Evil Genius of the Third Crusade': Conrad of Montferrat, stereotype and scapegoat** 60
MARIANNE M^cLEOD GILCHRIST

5 **Saladin and Richard the Lionheart: entangled memories** 75
MIKE HORSWELL

6 Saint Louis: a crusader king and hero for Victorian and
   First World War Britain and Ireland   95
   ELIZABETH SIBERRY

7 The sultan, the Kaiser, the colonel, and the purloined wreath 112
   CAROLE HILLENBRAND

   Index   125

Figures

5.1	Figures believed to be Richard and Saladin jousting, Luttrell Psalter, *British Library*, BL Add MS 42130, fol. 82, *c.* 1325–1335	79
5.2	Gustave Doré, 'Richard Cœur De Lion A La Bataille D'Arsur' in Joseph François Michaud, *Histoire des Croisades,* vol. 1 (Paris, 1877), pp. 368–69	80
5.3	Cameo brooch from *c.* 1850s featuring the combat of Richard and Saladin from Abraham Cooper's 1828 painting	81
6.1	St Louis in a window designed by Louis Davis	103
6.2	Memorial window, All Saints, Darfield	105
7.1	Exterior of Saladin's mausoleum, Damascus. Image by Jan Smith	113
7.2	Saladin's coffins, Damascus	114
7.3	Plaque on Saladin's coffin, Damascus	115
7.4	The Kaiser's wreath, Imperial War Museum London, EPH 4338	117
7.5	The Kaiser's wreath, Imperial War Museum	118
7.6	Imperial German eagle employed until 1918	119
7.7	Detail of Arabic inscription below the Kaiser's monogram, from Figure 7.4	120
7.8	Detail of Arabic quotation at the bottom of the wreath, from Figure 7.4	121

Acknowledgements

The editors of the fourth volume in the series *Engaging the Crusades* would like to thank all those who presented papers in the strands we organised at the International Medieval Congress at Leeds in July 2018, some of whose papers are developed here. As always, the final artefact represents but the tip of the iceberg and this has been a collaborative effort. We would like to espcieally thank the contributors who have diligently written and made edits amidst the challenges of the global pandemic. We would also like to thank Jonathan Phillips for continuing encouragement and support for the project, Laura Pilsworth, Morwenna Scott and Isabel Voice at Routledge, as well as James Arlett, Giovanna Di Rosa, Philip Jackson, Merav Mack, Simon Parsons, Iris Shagrir, Johannes Frankow, and Stephen Spencer for various contributions to the process of bringing this book together. As ever, Mike would like to thank Lauren for her enthusiasm and patience with, the production of this volume, and Robyn and Theo for welcome distractions.

Abbreviations

CUP   Cambridge University Press
MUP   Manchester University Press
OUP   Oxford University Press

Frequently used references:

Engaging the Crusades, Vol. 1   Mike Horswell and Jonathan Phillips, eds., *Perceptions of the Crusades from the Nineteenth to the Twenty-First Century: Engaging the Crusades, Volume One* (Abingdon: Routledge, 2018)

Hollywood in the Holy Land   Nickolas Haydock and Edward L. Risden eds., *Hollywood in the Holy Land: Essays on Film Depictions of the Crusades and Christian-Muslim Clashes* (London: McFarland & Company, 2009)

Phillips, *Saladin*   Jonathan Phillips, *The Life and Legend of the Sultan Saladin.* (London: Bodley Head, 2019)

Runciman, *History*   Steven Runciman, *A History of the Crusades,* 3 vols (Cambridge: CUP, 1951–4)

Siberry, *New Crusaders*   Elizabeth Siberry, *The New Crusaders: Images of the Crusades in the 19th and Early 20th Centuries* (Aldershot: Ashgate, 2000)

Contributors

John D. Cotts is Professor of History at Whitman College, USA and author of *The Clerical Dilemma: Peter of Blois and Literate Culture in the Twelfth Century* (2009) and *Europe's Long Twelfth Century: Order, Anxiety, and Adaptation 1095–1229* (2013). He is currently working on biblical exegesis and ideology at the time of the Third Crusade.

Marianne McLeod Gilchrist is a historian and art historian, currently working as a historical/heritage consultant and teacher in lifelong learning. She is a Fellow of the Society of Antiquaries of Scotland and has written on a variety of subjects, including *Patrick Ferguson: 'A Man of Some Genius'* (2003). She has a strong interest in inter-relationships between historiography, history painting, and literature, about which she has published in the *Journal of Historical Fictions*. She has been researching Conrad of Montferrat and his representation in historiography, fiction, and film for some years.

Carole Hillenbrand (CBE, FBA, FRSE) is Professor Emerita of Islamic History at Edinburgh University and Professorial Fellow of Islamic History at St Andrews, Scotland. She is the author of *The Crusades: Islamic Perspectives* (1999). Her special research interests also include the history of the Seljuq Turks and Islamic political thought.

Mike Horswell is the author of *The Rise and Fall of British Crusader Medievalism, c. 1825–1945* (2018) and has taught at Royal Holloway (University of London), King's College London, and the University of Oxford, UK. He is a Fellow of the Royal Historical Society and is currently researching, teaching, and writing about the memory and use of the crusades in the modern era.

Danielle E.A. Park is an Honorary Research Associate at the University of York and lectures in Medieval History at Royal Holloway, UK. Her book, *Papal Protection and the Crusader: Flanders, Champagne, and the*

Kingdom of France, 1095–1222, was published in 2018. She appeared on BBC Radio's *In Our Time* to discuss Queen Melisende of Jerusalem and is currently researching a monograph on the reign of Melisende and Fulk in Jerusalem (1131–61) for the Routledge series Rulers of the Latin East.

Francesca Petrizzo is working on a biography and cultural history of Tancred, Prince of Antioch and has recently completed a Leverhulme Study Abroad project at the Università di Roma Tor Vergata, Italy. She is based at the University of Leeds, UK, and works on kin, identity, and culture at war in the Middle Ages, and on the medievalisms of political movements between the early modern and modern eras.

Elizabeth Siberry is a researcher whose current work examines how families memorialised the crusades and crusading ancestors through legend, art, and architecture, and the reception of the crusades in the nineteenth century. She has published many articles and chapters on nineteenth- and twentieth-century images of the crusades in Britain, most notably in her book *The New Crusaders* (2000).

Kristin Skottki is Junior Professor of Medieval History at the University of Bayreuth, Germany. She has published on the medieval and modern historiography of the First Crusade in her monograph *Christen, Muslime und der Erste Kreuzzug* (2015). Her current research focuses on late medieval piety and medievalism.

Introduction
Making heroes and villains

Mike Horswell and Kristin Skottki

What's in a hero (or villain)?

Felix Heinzer, Jörn Leonhard and Ralf von den Hoff offer a helpful overview over the different dimensions that need to be considered when analysing the hero and the heroic:

> People are considered heroic figures […] if they perform an *extraordinary achievement* in an 'agonal'[1] context or if such an achievement can be ascribed to them, or even a capability that goes beyond the human scale. This achievement must be *narrated*, it can only become a heroic deed or a special quality of the hero in the mediation. This mediation – in whatever medium – constitutes the hero in his connection to the *audience*. Heroes are therefore created by [and for] their audiences, they fascinate them; heroes are imitated, admired or revered by a following, but are also critically evaluated or opposed by others: heroes therefore *polarise*, they evoke fascination and amazement as well as rejection. They force us to relate to them: this is precisely where their special effect lies on processes of endowment with meaning, self-enlightenment and the collective discussion of norms in societies. The heroic is thus an attributed category of the extraordinary; processes of denial and attribution of this quality must be investigated. Heroicisations mark the crossing of boundaries and, as cultural practices, are components of the collective discussion of conflicts over the scope of norms and values. *In them, societies and social groups struggle for their self-interpretation and negotiate their boundaries.*[2]

Thus, no one was ever born a hero or a villain – heroes and villains are what one may become, what others may turn one into. Processes of heroisation are socially constructed and embodied: studying them reveals the mutability of reputation, historical transformations, and methods of translation.

Recent research into the construction of the hero and the heroic also shows that especially for the era often called 'the Middle Ages', no single, homogeneous concept of the heroic was prevalent. Depending on the social strata of society of the producers and recipients of the stories about heroes and villains (lay, courtly, ecclesiastical, urban, etc.) and the medial and narrative frame of these stories (*chanson de geste*, historiography, illustration, liturgy, etc.), we may encounter very different and sometimes even contradicting concepts of the heroic.[3]

Ulrich Bröckling named four dimensions of the heroic, which suggest the crusades are a perfect setting for heroic behaviour: morally regulated deviation, honour or veneration, agency, and a willingness to make sacrifices.[4] A crusade hero could, for example, challenge the order of the battle, the mutually agreed hierarchy in leadership, or even abandon (temporarily) the original objective of the crusade, but all for the sake of a higher gain, the victory in a hopeless combat, or even for the glory of Christ. Bohemund of Taranto's self-fashioning as a crusade hero illustrates this.[5] The battles and conquests during the crusades presented a 'field of honour' and a perfect space to deploy 'agonal' agency; after all, all crusaders were not only prepared to make sacrifices, but even face death, as the remission of sins was the highest gain to be won by dying on crusade. But the crusades also offered many opportunities and possibilities for failing, disappointing or even sabotaging the ideals of 'holy war' – and therefore to become a crusade villain. For Bröckling the villain exemplifies the counterpart of the hero in the field of morally regulated deviation:

> In this counter type the moral portents are reversed. The figures to be assigned to this type undoubtedly have greatness, but this is manifested in evil, or more precisely: in what is considered shameful and villainous according to the prevailing heroic code. Instead of admirable heroic deeds, they commit despicable misdeeds, or at least they are accused of doing so. They may be exceptional, but they are anything but a role model; not an example, but a scandal.[6]

But still, the villain is part of the sacralised sphere of the heroic – people hearing or reading of the deeds of the villain or the hero cannot stay indifferent; they may admire or reject, worship, or even hate these figures, which is due to the polarising power of heroic semantics.[7]

The processes of ascribing heroism to certain figures may of course also change over time, especially if the norms and values of a given society change. This is particularly true for three features of the heroic: (1) the moral or political ambiguity, (2) the violence or 'agonal' power, and (3) the masculinity of the hero.

Morality

Striking in the research on heroism is the ambiguity and ambivalence of the heroic. Medievalist literary studies especially have shown that ambiguity and ambivalence, even 'fragility' of the hero and the heroic narrative, seem to be a feature of medieval imaginations of the heroic.[8] The 'hero' therefore cannot simply be understood as the embodiment of 'perfect goodness' in an ethical sense, as he often transgresses or even violates ethical norms by his exorbitant power. Heroes are definitely not 'normal'; their deeds 'oscillate [...] between norm-formation, norm-fulfilment, and norm-violation; between exceptionality and exemplarity'.[9] This tension may also be seen in the ambivalence of the hero as an individual, historical person on the one hand and as a supratemporal type of character/figure on the other.[10]

But more importantly, the deeds of the hero might be judged by some as condemnable and by others as righteous: 'Hero or villain, hero or traitor, these are always political issues as well: one's liberation hero is a terrorist to another, what is treason to one side is a revelation of state crimes to another.'[11] Ascribing heroic (or villainous) qualities to a certain person has to be done by a society or group – it is always a social act, embodied in particular communities. Heroisation requires a heroic discourse, practices, and institutions of venerating the hero, as well as media (re-)producing the heroic narrative. The hero for one group might nevertheless still be challenged as a villain by others – an obvious example might be Charlemagne, who was and is admired by some as the exemplary defender and utterer of the Christian faith, while he is despised by others as a blood-thirsty fanatic and slayer of the Saxons.[12] This oscillating effect of the hero probably also turned Charlemagne into one of the most important paragons of the crusading movement in songs and literature of the High and Late Middle Ages.[13]

Violence

If a society or a group develops other attitudes towards war and especially towards sacralised violence (i.e. the idea of so-called 'holy war'), as can be seen with the images and judgments of the crusades through the centuries, then the image and assessment of alleged crusading heroes (and villains) will unavoidably change as well. As today sacralised violence is often condemned as 'medieval' and abhorrent by most majority and mainstream societies, crusade heroes, as well as other heroic figures whose reputation was built on their military prowess and violent self-assertion, are rarely understood as heroes anymore. Nevertheless, in some 'subcultural' parts of these societies (be they White Supremacists or Islamists), crusaders or their opponents such as Saladin, respectively, might still be venerated as liberation heroes.[14]

Gender

One of the most persistent features of the heroic is that it is almost exclusively framed by ideas of masculinity.[15] Masculinity is understood not as a 'natural', given, attribute of the male sex, but rather as a category of performance and achievement. But what is considered masculine is also subject to historical change. It is therefore unsurprising that popular perceptions today usually imagine crusaders to be male. Crusader Studies has only recently openly addressed the different roles of women in the crusades, and how much the image of crusading itself is driven by gendered assumptions.[16]

Creating crusading heroes and villains

The authors of the chapters in this volume consider heroism and its obverse, villainy, as constructed narratives rather than natural features of the world. In interrogating the ways in which crusading heroes and villains have been assembled they seek to understand the contexts which have created, sustained, or refashioned them – and often reflect back on perceptions of the crusading enterprise as a whole. Addressing the legacy of one of the First Crusade's key figures, the Southern Italian Norman Tancred, Francesca Petrizzo has examined the ways in which Tancred's attributes have been variously represented in the past nine centuries to present an anatomy of a hero's memory. Tancred's starring role in Torquato Tasso's epic poem *Gerusalemme liberata* (1591) has affected all subsequent appearances of the crusader, and Petrizzo dissects the ways in which his recorded actions and attributes have been interpreted in subsequent portrayals.

Tackling a 'forgotten' crusading figure, Danielle E.A. Park has traced the memorialisation of Queen Melisende of Jerusalem (r. 1131–61) into the present, highlighting the ways in which Melisende has been overshadowed or only obliquely addressed. Park's critical analysis of Judith Tarr's *Queen of Swords* (1997) is a deep engagement with a complex depiction of Melisende. Park finds a proto-feminist model of rulership relevant to the late twentieth century, and her chapter suggests that the gendered nature of assumptions about heroism have left a legacy in how heroes are configured and who is remembered as such.

Two subsequent chapters consider the construction of villainy. John D. Cotts' chapter focuses on the ways in which a traditional villain, Reynald of Châtillon (*c.* 1125–87), has been presented. Often rendered a foil for Saladin's chivalry, and most notably featuring in Ridley Scott's film *Kingdom of Heaven* (2005) as a practitioner of exorbitant violence, Reynald's reputation has found defenders. Cotts' exploration of the variations of Reynald's villainy illustrates its plasticity. Similarly, Marianne McLeod Gilchrist historicises the reputation of Conrad of Montferrat (d.

1192) through a consideration of his presentation in literature and film in the modern era. Conrad has suffered at the hands of authors and scriptwriters who have found him useful as an antagonist, and in so doing have repeated the stereotypes and prejudices of earlier ages.

The final three chapters contribute further fresh approaches to the topic. Rather than concentrating on the reputation of a single figure, Mike Horswell considers the fictional encounters of Richard 'the Lionheart' and Salah al-Din ibn Ayyub, known to the West as Saladin. While considerations of each individually abound, the entanglement of the two in the Third Crusade (1189–92) presents the potential for a dynamic encounter; imagined meetings of two 'heroes' reveals the desires of their creators. Elizabeth Siberry's chapter breaks down the traditional national compartmentalising of heroic figures – especially royal ones – by demonstrating the ways in which St Louis IX, king of France (1214–70), also functioned as a chivalric exemplar for the British and Irish in the Victorian and Edwardian periods. This chapter shows that historical memories of figures – heroes, villains, and others – have utility beyond their 'home' contexts and of the importance of locating memories within specific, historical communities.

In reconsidering the bronze wreath laid at the tomb of Saladin in Damascus in 1898 by Kaiser Wilhelm II, the German Emperor (1859–1941), Carole Hillenbrand presents an accurate translation of all the inscriptions for the first time. Coupling the words with a visual interpretation of the symbolism of the wreath, Hillenbrand argues that the only emperor the Kaiser recognised was himself, and that his gift was designed to elevate Saladin's memory in order to place himself above it. As well as situating the Kaiser's wreath more accurately in its contemporary context, Hillenbrand also demonstrates the mutability of memory and its multiple entanglements by offering a *new* translation of an artefact which has spent a century in the Imperial War Museum after being removed by T.E. Lawrence during the First World War. In so doing, the chapter reveals the links between materiality, memory, and propaganda.

This book is clearly unable to address all the possible characters associated with the crusades and their heterogeneous reception across multiple historical contexts. Godfrey of Bouillon, a leader of the First Crusade, was celebrated as an exemplary Christian knight and king as one of the Nine Worthies, and later came to be appropriated by the modern nations of Germany, France, and Belgium. Saladin's memory is prominent and flexibly invoked but what about Baybars and Zengi? Rather, the editors hope it will start conversations, not least about the silences and omissions in public memory and about what 'counts' as a 'crusading hero' or 'villain', and why. This volume begins to trace out and 'relentlessly historicise' the reputation and memories of figures inextricably associated with the crusades and who, in turn, exert influence on that memory.[17]

Notes

1 We use this technical term as it is central to the academic discussion of medieval heroism – a fitting English translation might be 'militant, combative, pugnacious, strident, warlike' in contexts of war, or battle, but also power, sovereignty, and sway.
2 Felix Heinzer, Jörn Leonhard, and Ralf von den Hoff, 'Einleitung: Relationen zwischen Sakralisierungen und Heroisierungen' in *Sakralität und Heldentum*, eds. Felix Heinzer, Jörn Leonhard, Ralf von den Hoff (Würzburg, 2017), p. 9. Translated by Kristin Skottki as in all following cases.
3 For an overview, see Ronald G. Asch et al., 'Das Heroische in der neueren kulturhistorischen Forschung. Ein kritischer Bericht', *H-Soz-Kult* (28 July 2015), <www.hsozkult.de/literaturereview/id/forschungsberichte-2216>, [accessed 12 February 2020].
4 Ulrich Bröckling, 'Negationen des Heroischen – ein typologischer Versuch', *helden. heroes. héros*. 3:1 (2015), p. 10.
5 As is shown by Ingrid Schlegl, 'Bohemund von Tarent. Konstruktion eines Idealbild Kreuzzugshelden' in *Heroes: Repräsentationen des Heroischen in Geschichte, Literatur und Alltag*, eds. Johanna Rolshoven, Toni Janosch Krause, and Justin Winkler (Bielefeld, 2018), pp. 383–405.
6 Bröckling, 'Negationen des Heroischen', p. 10.
7 Ibid.
8 See Anne-Katrin Federow, Kay Malcher, and Marina Münkler, eds., *Brüchige Helden - brüchiges Erzählen. Mittelhochdeutsche Heldenepik aus narratologischer Sicht* (Berlin and Boston, 2017).
9 Ulrich Bröckling, 'Negationen des Heroischen, p. 9.
10 Ibid., p. 13.
11 Bröckling, 'Negationen des Heroischen', p. 11. See also Johanna Rolshoven, 'Helden 2.0: Zur Einleitung' in Rolshoven, Krause, and Winkler (eds.), *Heroes*, p. 13.
12 See Matthew Gabriele, and Jace Stuckey, eds., *The Legend of Charlemagne in the Middle Ages: Power, Faith, and Crusade* (New York, 2008).
13 Of the broad literature on the Chanson de Roland (and its translations and transmissions) see William J. Purkis, and Matthew Gabriele, eds., *The Charlemagne Legend in Medieval Latin Texts* (Cambridge, 2016).
14 See Mike Horswell and Akil N. Awan, eds., *The Crusades in the Modern World: Engaging the Crusades, Volume Two* (Abingdon, 2019) and forthcoming volumes on contemporary appropriations of the crusades.
15 But see the differentiating contributions in Carolin Hauck, Monika Mommertz, Andreas Schlüter, and Thomas Seedorf, eds., *Tracing the Heroic through Gender* (Baden-Baden, 2018).
16 Susan B. Edgington, and Sarah Lambert, eds., *Gendering the Crusades* (Cardiff, 2001); Ingrid Baumgärtner, and Melanie Panse, 'Kreuzzüge aus der Perspektive der Genderforschung. Zielsetzung und Forschungsansätze', *Das Mittelalter: Perspektiven Mediävistischer Forschung* 21:1 (2016), pp. 1–18.
17 Kristin Skottki, 'The Dead, the Revived and the Recreated Pasts: "Structural Amnesia" in Representations of Crusade History' in *Engaging the Crusades, Vol. 1*, p. 124.

1 'Most Excellent and Brave of Heart'

Tancred's making and unmaking in the sources[1]

Francesca Petrizzo

Introduction: a young, antagonistic, able military leader

For Edward Gibbon, writing in 1788, Tancred, one of the crusader conquerors of Jerusalem in 1099, was a man of 'accomplished character' in whom one could 'discover all the virtues of a perfect knight'.[2] For David Douglas, writing nearly 200 years later in 1976, Tancred was instead 'hard, unlovable, unscrupulous and intensely able [...], personally repellent.'[3] The fault line between these two historical judgments perfectly charts the conflict in Tancred's legacy: that between a hero of the crusader movement and one of its villains. By focusing thematically on how the crucial elements of his depiction could be framed differently in narratives of praise or disapproval, this chapter will show how Tancred, both the youngest and one of the most successful crusader leaders, typifies the evolution and the fall of the model of heroic crusader behaviour. His undoubtedly efficient wars as a young knight can be shown to represent the highest achievements of Christian holy war, or to denounce its crusades' darkest sides. The portrayal of Tancred remains remarkably consistent through the centuries: sources reliably emphasise his very young age at the time of the crusade, his passionate and often hot-tempered character, and his remarkable ability in war. The way these constant characteristics could be depicted, however, varies widely, making him a particularly suitable case study in framing his image by tracking a larger trend – the rise and fall of the idea of crusade – as an example both of extreme heroism and of profound villainy.

A short summary of his career in Outremer immediately identifies Tancred as a highly effective operator within the crusader movement: probably still in his late teens when he joined the expedition to the East in 1097, within 15 years Tancred accrued considerable power and achieved a position of pre-eminence before his sudden death of illness in early December 1112, when he was probably not yet 35.[4] A son of the Northern Italian Odo the Good Marquis and of the Southern Norman Emma, and a grandson of the notorious Robert Guiscard, Tancred was one of the leaders of the First Crusade and one of the most prominent noblemen of the newly born Latin Kingdom of Jerusalem. He had first been the lieutenant of his uncle Bohemond, had then served Raymond of St Gilles, and had finally become a close collaborator of Godfrey of Bouillon, who made him prince of Galilee. Embroiled in a lifelong enmity with Baldwin, Tancred consistently crossed, and was crossed by, Bohemond, but he was still left in charge of Antioch by his uncle when he went to Europe to raise an anti-Byzantine expedition, while it was with Baldwin that Tancred reached the edges of the Euphrates in a push against the Kingdom of Jerusalem's neighbours. While Bohemond swore loyalty to Byzantium after his defeat by the Empire in 1108, Tancred refused to respect the treaty, and at his death in 1112 he was undefeated by the Empire and engaged in successful war against his closest Muslim neighbour, Ridwan of Aleppo.[5]

Alongside his ability to accumulate and defend territorial gains, Tancred cultivated a consistently antagonistic attitude towards his contemporaries and got into disputes with both his enemies and his allies. In early narratives of the crusades, Tancred is a striking figure; and in later fictional reworkings and scholarly interpretations, he is an idiosyncratic and often divisive one. Closing in on the textual depictions of Tancred's life, be it historical or literary accounts, quickly allows us to see how such an evolution came to be codified. We can trace it through writing from the earliest medieval accounts of the crusade, into early modern poetry, to the evolution of modern historiography from the eighteenth century onward, until the rise of the modern novel from the nineteenth to the twenty-first century. This chapter will, accordingly, investigate the Latin, Greek, and Arabic sources for the First Crusade, beginning with those written by Tancred's contemporaries in the late eleventh and early twelfth century, progressing to those compiled throughout the twelfth century and their reworkings in *chanson* form. The chapter will then tackle the immensely influential legacy of Torquato Tasso's *Gerusalemme liberata*, a sixteenth-century Italian poem on the First Crusade whose wild popularity across Europe in the following centuries made Tancred an enduringly popular symbol of crusader heroism; of Tancred, Tasso wrote, 'There is none […] more excellent and brave of heart.'[6] Finally, the chapter will conclude with an examination of a selection of nineteenth, twentieth, and twenty-first century novels, which, with the rise of adult literacy in Europe and the advent of widely known modern historiography, allowed Tancred's representations to become both more diverse and more emblematic of the sea-change in perceptions of the crusader movement as a whole.

Modern historiographical attitudes to Tancred's character have been layered, showing him to be a polarising figure in history as well as in fiction.

Older historians, such as Gibbon, or the French Joseph François Michaud, who wrote in the early nineteenth century, accepted Tasso's vision of a young and chivalrous knight, with Michaud intently referencing Tasso throughout his writing on the First Crusade.[7] This was followed by more sober but still quite balanced accounts in the writings of nineteenth- and early twentieth-century historians, such as Bernhard Kugler and Ralph Yewdale, who acknowledged Tancred's efficiency and ambitious behaviour; these assessments have been echoed by Claude Cahen, writing in the 1940s, and more recently by Tom Asbridge.[8] This seam of balanced assessments leaves behind the earlier depiction of Tancred as a crusader hero. But it was the 1940s and '50s, with the writing of Robert Nicholson (1940) and, most influentially, of Steven Runciman (1951), that marked a sharp reversal in Tancred's fortune and firmly redefined popular perceptions of him as an unlikeable and loathsome member of the crusader movement, crucially influencing contemporary representations, and a further evolution of his legacy, within the larger fortunes of the crusader era.[9]

'The Ferocious and Graceful Young Man': Tancred's youth

The most prominent leaders of the First Crusade were men in their 30s and 40s: Godfrey of Bouillon, Bohemond of Taranto, and Baldwin of Boulogne.[10] It is unsurprising that Tancred, who was probably still in his late teens, should stand out. Immediately entrusted with the command of part of Bohemond's army when it crossed from Southern Italy to the Balkans, Tancred, the crusader leader who succeeded in escaping swearing Alexios' oath in Byzantium, established himself for his effectiveness in spite of his years.[11] While by dint of superior manpower Baldwin expelled him from Tarsus, Tancred's capture of the city upon splitting from the main crusader army in Asia Minor is an early testimony to both his acquisitiveness and efficiency in pursuing what would become a lifelong expansion campaign.[12]

Of the early twelfth-century chroniclers of the First Crusade it is unsurprising, then, that Tancred's biographer Ralph of Caen should insist that Tancred was already more than a match for his peers in his adolescence, and wiser than much older men.[13] To Albert of Aachen, Tancred was a *tyro illustris*, a 'prominent young knight', remarkable both because of his youth and his high standing.[14] Guibert of Nogent saw in Tancred's age a graceful touch: it was due to his 'youthful impatience' that Tancred couldn't abide his elders' lengthy counsels, interrupting their speeches.[15] That Tancred's youth was well known is underscored by the fact that the texts attesting to it have separate origins. Tancred's contemporaries seem to have found in his age a very distinctive trait, and it is consistently present in early accounts of the crusade from this time. While Tancred is a very minor character in the Old French crusader cycle, appearing with any amount of prominence only in the *Chanson d'Antioche* and the *Chanson de Jérusalem*, it was in the sixteenth century that he received his most enduring representation.[16]

Torquato Tasso's 1581 poem *Gerusalemme liberata* is a work in Italian *ottava rima* (the most popular metre for chivalric poems, in stanzas of 8 lines of 10 or 11 syllables), a celebration of the First Crusade in 20 *canti* heavily influenced by the wildly popular *Orlando furioso* by Lodovico Ariosto (1516–32). A fictionalised account of the crusade featuring sorcerers, enchantments, and prophecies, the work was still defended by its author as being firmly based in a careful perusal of the original sources.[17] The sources of Tasso are a complex issue: we know, however, that he used both Robert the Monk and William of Tyre, and Vincenzo Vivaldi and Michael Murrin make a strong case for his also having known and used Albert of Aachen, something which I find conclusively established by his depiction of Tancred.[18] While Franco Cardini insists that the Tassian and historical Tancred 'only share a name', Tasso's Tancredi has many of the characteristics of the figure sketched out by the sources, who lent a few distinguishing traits to Rinaldo, the other young knight of Tasso's epic.[19] Youth is a fundamental characteristic of the chivalric hero: Tasso's investment in a historical basis for his character adhered to the contemporary ideal of 'truthful' poetry, a raging debate in the Italian intellectual environment of his time, and found in the impetuous and adolescent Tancred of the chronicles an ideal match.[20]

Tasso's depictions of Tancred insist on his youth and accompanying attributes: a smooth face, a lithe body, and a boyish beauty are constantly insisted upon. Tasso's Tancredi is a 'ferocious and graceful young man', whose beauty is delicate, and whose slender if powerful body firmly sets him apart from older warriors, such as the Muslim Argante.[21] That youth is fundamental to Tasso's idea of a hero is underscored by Rinaldo. If Tancredi is young, Rinaldo is younger: a rebellious hero in the legacy of Achilles, Rinaldo is described, like Tancredi, as beautiful yet powerful, a boy hero who first plants the standard of the Cross on Jerusalem's walls (with Tancredi following a moment later, respecting the fact that the historical Tancred was among the first beyond the walls with Godfrey's force).[22] Tasso's choice of Tancred as one of the three heroes of the poem (together with Rinaldo and Goffredo, a fictionalisation of Godfrey of Bouillon) anchors his narrative to history at the same time as allowing him to cleave to a staple of chivalric literature.

Tasso's widespread fortune consecrated the image of Tancred as a beautiful youth. In artistic depictions of scenes from the poem by sixteenth- and seventeenth-century masters such as Tintoretto, Poussin, and Ricchi, Tancredi is a slender warrior with delicate features and curly locks.[23] It was after Tancredi that in 1760 Voltaire named his *Tancrède*, a fictional

Sicilian hero slighted but righteous and ultimately tragically victorious.²⁴ Voltaire's play was then adapted, and further spread, by Rossini's opera *Tancredi* (first performed in 1813 in Venice).²⁵ The composer significantly wrote the lead role for a female contralto, a common device used in opera for young heroes, and which Rossini in particular also used in *La donna del lago* (1819) and *Semiramide* (1823): in opera, as in Renaissance chivalric poetry, Tancred fit neatly into a tradition of young, beautiful heroes as standard-bearers of virtue.²⁶ In 1847 Disraeli named his novel *Tancred* after its protagonist, a young and passionate English lord who goes to seek spiritual enlightenment in the East, and who is once more a handsome, chivalrous model of heroic goodness.²⁷ Modern depictions of Tancred have sometimes espoused this depiction: David Donachie's *Crusades* series (2013–14) accompanies Tancred from childhood to the siege of Antioch, depicting him as Bohemond's protégé, first as a sweet-faced squire who gets in trouble for courting girls, then as a handsome, tall young man who matches his impressive uncle.²⁸ In his popular history of the First Crusade (2004), Asbridge sketched out Tancred as 'tall, blond and powerfully built' on the model of his uncle, testifying to the enduring power of the image of Tancred as a handsome youth.²⁹

But if on the one hand youth can be used as shorthand for beauty and purity, on the other it can entail immaturity. Sini Kangas has underscored how youthful language in crusader sources can indicate not just age, but also a very junior rank, and the taint of someone simply too inexperienced.³⁰ Ralph of Caen could not solve the tension between his desire to praise the prince he had served and his junior status at the time of the First Crusade: one of the final scenes in his unfinished work shows Bohemond sharply reminding Tancred that he is just not important enough to command the attention of European royalty in attempting to raise a crusade.³¹

The idea that a young hero is also, fundamentally, a hero with much to learn, and one unable to act as he should, accompanies and often complicates depictions of Tancred. When Ascanio Grandi set out to praise a hero of his own land, Southern Italy, with the 1632 poem *Tancredi*, he significantly did so by aligning his representation of Tancred with that of the classical hero Aeneas: a righteous man in his 30s, his Tancred is still handsome enough to make the Empress Mathilde fall in love with him on sight, but he also has the wisdom and experience of age.³² The tropes of youth, boyish beauty, and impetuosity are instead bestowed on Tancred's fictional son Idro.³³ If, however, the luminous youth of Tasso's Tancredi long eclipsed these connotations, modern writers have often built on the less positive aspects of Tancred's youth.

In Giuseppe Tomasi di Lampedusa's 1958 novel *The Leopard*, the hero, Tancredi Falconeri, is the penniless scion of Sicilian nobility who marries money and feigns revolutionary sympathies to climb the social ladder of the newly born Kingdom of Italy.[34] While the name immediately evokes Tasso's chivalric hero, lending a noble gloss to the character, Falconeri is a winsome but ultimately acerbic man: a character whose early promise remains empty, and whose life ends in a disappointing marriage and a hollow career. And while Tomasi di Lampedusa was building on the literary associations of Tancred's name, historical writers of the same period employed the less savoury associations of youth to great effect in their own narratives. Laverne Gay's meticulously researched *Wine of Satan* (1949) shows her hero, Bohemund, as a poised, mature man, and makes of Tancred's age a boundary-blurring trait.[35] In the course of the novel, Tancred's growing can be tracked by the scars that bely his prettiness, and the twist with which the years make his mouth 'hard and firm', as the brutality of the crusader enterprise takes its toll.[36] To Gay, youth's purity is illusory and a decoy, and Tancred's progressive ruin a litmus test for the crusade's cost. And while Alfred Duggan's Tancred in his 1964 novel has a masculine beauty (both he and Bohemond are described as strikingly tall and handsome) his youth carries with it the affectation of long hair 'in the Lombard fashion', and an ideological lack of nuance bordering on bigotry.[37] Tancred is shown as a fanatically faithful young Christian, one with a blunt code of honour, but also with a zealous enthusiasm in killing 'infidels'. He embodies for Duggan the excesses of the crusade, despite his uncle's attempts at educating him to a subtler view of the world.[38]

The association between Tancred's youth and ferocious violence is capitalised upon by Edwin Thomas, who makes of it a severe indictment against the crusader movement in his novels *Knights of the Cross* (2006) and *Siege of Heaven* (2007).[39] Thomas's hero, Byzantine clerk Demetrios Askiates, undertakes a series of investigations into conspiracy and murder during the First Crusade. The series as a whole makes a stand against the idea of Christian war, showing the Western knights, by and large, as opportunistic, predatory, and religiously intolerant.[40] Among them, Tancred stands out as a particularly unnerving and terrifying villain. Tancred's childishly high-pitched voice and young, acne-ridden and beardless face are a turn of the screw on his conscienceless killing: the novel shows him unblinkingly torturing prisoners and engaging in cheerful cannibalism to terrify the Turks, his boyish looks a frightful inconsistency for the horrified Demetrios, who cannot reconcile Tancred's apparent innocence with his monstrous nature.[41]

Tancred's youth, then, which was a distinguishing trait for several of his contemporaries, has served to both align him with the idealised hero of crusader celebration and to signify immaturity and lack of depth, making him a particularly useful figure to denounce the horror of holy war. And youth's potential for immaturity tallies well with another trait constantly accompanying him: an enduring and often passionate display of emotion.

'He Was Extremely Angry When He Saw This': Tancred's character

Tancred was consistently depicted by his contemporaries as a man with a very short temper, subject to fits of anger. In the terse words of the anonymous author of the *Gesta Francorum*, Tancred 'was extremely angry' when he saw that the prisoners to whom he had given his banner for protection had been murdered in Jerusalem; the same episode caused Albert of Aachen's unrelated chronicle to denounce his immaturity, joining youth and a short temper in the depiction of a hot-headed young man.[42] For the Byzantine historian Anna Komnene, writing around 1148, Tancred's excessive rage was a fundamental part of his being a 'man of independent spirit' to the point of behaving like a 'drunken wastrel'.[43] She described with disdain Tancred's boldness in attempting to upbraid the Emperor Alexios, lingering on his impertinence in asking for the imperial tent as a gift for swearing fealty. While Anna depicts Bohemond as an impressive man and a worthy adversary of the Empire, to her, Tancred's inability to control his outbursts marks him as troublesome.[44] That his anger was well known and held against Tancred is shown by Ralph of Caen's efforts in transforming it into something praiseworthy. The outburst against the emperor is described by Ralph as a righteous harangue against excessive imperial power.[45] When Arnulf of Chocques, Ralph's own mentor and thus a particularly sore source of criticism, tells off Tancred for greed, Ralph has his hero reply that 'it is not my words, but my sword and spear that recommend me', sublimating his anger into a warlike lack of diplomacy.[46]

Tancred's anger and his willingness to seek his personal advantage at all cost – constantly repeated in the sources – seem to amount to the coherent depiction of a man unwilling to countenance any delay at obtaining his objectives, and apparently incapable of restraining his displeasure when thwarted. This percolated into later representations of the crusade: it was Tancred's excessive anger at Baldwin that Bohemond upbraided in the *Chanson d'Antioche*.

Tasso capitalised on descriptions of Tancred's anger, lending it to Rinaldo. The young hero's disagreement with Goffredo leads to his temporarily abandoning the crusade and nearly dooming it.[47] It is Tancredi who attempts to talk Rinaldo down in the *Liberata*: with a twist on the tradition of Tancred's fury, Tancredi explains to Rinaldo how he had to put aside his rightful anger at Baldovino (Baldwin), who had stolen Tarsus from him, in order to prioritise the crusader cause over his personal grievance.[48] But if Tasso tempered Tancredi's anger, he also turned the historical character's seeming ability to feel strong emotion into his character's most memorable trait: erotic and melancholy passion.

Tancredi survives in popular memory chiefly thanks to a very fictional trait of his character, his doomed love for the Muslim warrior Clorinda.[49] His love for Clorinda makes Tancredi unfit for holy war: while he hotly declares his love of Christ before fearlessly facing down the apostate Rambaldo when alone, the sight of Clorinda is enough to petrify him and causes him to fail to fight as the champion for the Christian side against the powerful Argante.[50] It is by pursuing a woman he believes to be Clorinda that Tancredi leaves behind the Christian camp, contributing to its rout.[51]

Clorinda's death at the unrecognising Tancredi's hands then turns his passion into a deep melancholy, in which he contemplates suicide and becomes further unfit for war.[52] When confronted by enchanted fire, Tancredi jumps unhesitatingly into it, but when a bewitched tree speaks to him in the voice of Clorinda, he abandons the enterprise Goffredo sent him on, and the sword falls from his hand.[53] It is only at the end of the poem, with the taking of Jerusalem, the killing of Argante, and the seeming promise of new love with Erminia, a Muslim princess of Antioch who had fallen in love with his chivalry and beauty, that Tancredi seems to regain his heroism, rising bare but armed from his sickbed to defend the crusader camp.[54] Tancredi's depiction as a man seized by melancholy and love-madness places him squarely in the field of Baroque poetry, as indicated by Wells.[55] Yet it is not a stretch to see why it is specifically on Tancredi that Tasso bestowed this love-madness. Rinaldo is undone by pride and lust, not a love to turn his brain, but it is to Tancred's lack of control over his own emotions that Tancredi's 'folly of love' harkens back, as explicitly (if somewhat fancifully) claimed by Tasso.[56]

And while Tancredi's romantic character and his follies have enjoyed extensive fortune in Tasso's influential legacy of painting, poetry, and prose inspired by the *Liberata*, Tancred's anger has found a new place in the negative depictions of his character discussed earlier.[57] For both Duggan and Thomas in their novels, Tancred's short temper is an integral part of his character's flaws. Neither of them depicts Tancred as a strategist, but both, if to a different extent, show him to be a violent and thuggish man, one whose lack of control, mercy, and subtlety feed into each other. Discussing Tancred's anger, moreover, brings us to the final and most divisive point of his depiction – that of Tancred as a man of effective violence.

'One of the Strongest Men of His Age': Tancred's skill in war

On one thing all sources concerning Tancred agree: that his military ability was remarkable. Anna Komnene, who insisted on Tancred's unworthiness and excesses, still identified him as 'one of the strongest men of his age' and bemoaned the decision to send a weak Byzantine governor to fight him.[58] Albert of Aachen disliked Tancred's immaturity but still lamented his sudden death as the loss of 'the warlike, famous, [...] strongest conqueror of the Turks.'[59] While we can see the print of classical models in Ralph of Caen's insistence that Tancred could kill three Turks with one blow, his biographer's literary licence sits next to a near-unanimous chorus of acknowledgement of military ability.[60] By all accounts, Tancred was a most efficient wager of Christian holy war; his willingness and ability to engage in violence is both a key factor in his reputation among his contemporary sources and the most divisive element of his memory in later depictions of the First Crusade.

For the Christian writers of his time, Tancred's military prowess could excuse many faults. Albert affectionately called him *'frater'* in lamenting his death, showing Tancred's talent in holding the boundary of the kingdom of Jerusalem weighed ultimately heavier with him than the prince's many faults.[61] Tancred's successes in Antioch seem to be the only possible explanation for Fulcher of Chartres' fondness for him. Fulcher lapsed into poetry to describe how Tancred 'paid his fatal debt', betraying his strong feelings over the matter.[62] Perhaps the strongest tribute to Tancred comes from William of Tyre, writing in the late twelfth century. In a departure from his usually caustic style, William expended himself in endless praise for Tancred.[63] To William, Tancred embodied the best of crusader heroism, whichever his defects.

Understandably, Tancred's enemies did not feel quite so warmly about his military successes. To Muslim chroniclers of the crusades, Tancred was a scourge, an efficient Frankish warrior, who conquered their cities and seized their best warriors.[64] In Usama Ibn Munqidh's notoriously colourful writing, this military quality becomes a particularly devious kind of cruelty: according to him, Tancred, who had promised a young Muslim to spare him should he ever capture him, did release the boy in observance of his word, but immediately blinded him in one eye, to ensure he would never fight the Christians again.[65] Nor was it Muslims alone who were unsure that Tancred's word could be trusted. While Peter Tudebode, who is one of the earliest sources on the First Crusade, agreed with Albert of Aachen and the anonymous author of the *Gesta Francorum* that Tancred attempted to rescue a few civilians during the massacre at Jerusalem, for Tudebode it was Tancred himself who then turned on them and slaughtered them.[66]

But contemporary depictions of Tancred and his skill in war, whether positive or negative, framed his talent for war within his role as a ruler of the Latin East. To the author of the *Gesta Francorum*, Tancred was a generous and valiant leader, who allowed his men to impose on the Byzantines for food and shelter and rescued the rear-guard of the army from ambush at the river Vardar.⁶⁷ For Fulcher, William of Tyre, and Albert of Aachen, Tancred was one of the most efficient protectors of Jerusalem in Outremer. To both Anna Komnene and Usama Ibn Munqidh, he was a loathsome but undoubtedly threatening and influential enemy of their people. As stressed by Asbridge in his analysis of his reign, the historical Tancred was a successful strategist and ruler: he lifted Antioch out of the poverty and lack of defences in which Bohemond had left it when he stripped it of resources before heading for the West, and pushed it to its maximum territorial extension through the gains made in 11 years of tireless campaigns.⁶⁸ As far as we can see from contemporary sources, Tancred was not just effective at personally engaging in violence: he was also proficient in using it strategically to build and uphold his dominions and to rule his territories.

Memories of him, however, almost completely abandon this aspect of his career. The Tancred of later fiction, whether negative or positive, is not a ruler but a highly individualised, eternally junior knight. For Tasso, Tancredi's valour is part of his persona as a knight of the Cross, not a leader of men. He takes his orders from Goffredo: his glory is personal, not collective, and he seemingly has no true followers but his squire Vafrino.⁶⁹ While for Tasso his martial virtues reflect positively on him as a knight of chivalric poetry, modern novels have framed these skills in a different light, as the accessory (positive or negative) to other men's glory. In the novels by Gay, Duggan, Donachie, and Thomas, Tancred serves essentially as Bohemond's (sometimes Godfrey's) sidekick, a co-protagonist whose chief role is to assist the hero and be a less brilliant foil to him. Tancred's junior status and his youth are crucial to this depiction: his early, independent successes are not lingered upon. While Gay's Tancred does eventually set out independently, he fades out at the end of the novel, riding off into a future not described in the pages.⁷⁰ Duggan's Tancred is a blunt instrument of war in the much more expert hands of Bohemond: he gains independent rule and titles by the end of the novel, but Bohemond is still the hero, while his nephew is a somewhat self-important youth upon whom his uncle looks fondly.⁷¹ For Donachie, Tancred's escape from Alexios' oath is the fruit of a brilliant plan by Bohemond, and his uncle's encouragement of his independence.⁷² Thomas's Tancred has a monstrous talent for cruelty, but that cruelty is ultimately short-sighted and self-serving: it is deployed in fulfilment of other men's plans.⁷³

In these modern representations of Tancred we can see the characteristics of his figure blend into each other, with youth and lack of control combining with warrior prowess in making variations of a striking, but fundamentally secondary character, the brawn to accompany Bohemond of Taranto's far more subtle brains. While thus to his contemporaries Tancred's talent for war had marked him out as a man to follow (in horror or admiration, depending on the writer's point of view), Tasso's individualisation of his character was the gateway to a more isolated kind of warlike success, one coded according to the conventions of chivalric poems. Modern writers' evaluations of Tancred, then, subordinate this talent to older crusader leaders' plans, turning back to his youth and lack of control as signs of a character fundamentally lacking in independence and thus bringing full circle the trajectory of praise of his ability in wielding violence: no longer the sign of his often troublesome independence, but the fundamental measure of his practical value to older and more experienced leaders and their enterprises, right or wrong.

Conclusion: Tancred, the unmaking of a hero

Throughout this chapter I have charted the evolution of the perception of one crusader, Tancred, from the contemporary sources of his time to modern-day novels. Tancred, a figure defined by his precocious military and territorial successes, and by a well-known bad character, seems to have represented in his own time a particularly successful model of crusader heroism. To Latin chroniclers invested in the continuation of the Kingdom of Jerusalem, his tireless waging of holy war made him a useful and praiseworthy man on the edge of Christendom, and excused other concerns about his character. Greek and Arabic sources seem to share this perception of Tancred's ability, while understandably inverting their judgment. It is through this efficacy and ability that much of the secondary literature has read Tancred's role in the crusader movement: from nineteenth- and twentieth-century assessments by Kugler and Yewdale, to Cahen and Asbridge's work.[74]

While Tancred's role in Outremer was defined by his effectiveness as a ruler in Antioch, fictional representations of his figure focused on his earlier, better documented, and far more junior years. The *Chanson d'Antioche* and *Chanson de Jérusalem* did not linger on the early years of the Latin Kingdom of Jerusalem, when Tancred flourished, but on the sieges of Antioch (1097–8) and Jerusalem (1099), during which Tancred had fought as a valiant but still junior crusader. It is on his youth, and its usefulness as a signifier and narrative device, that Tasso built, consecrating the image of Tancred as an impeccably chivalrous – but extremely young and volatile – character. It is on this image that Michaud seized in his influential *Histoire des croisades*, which constantly referenced Tasso, perpetuating his legacy as the embodiment of crusader chivalry.[75]

At the same time, the popularity of Tancredi's romantic storylines eclipsed his ties with the historical Tancred, opening a gulf in perception between the historical person and his representations on which critics such as Salvatore Multineddu commented in disgust, disappointed that the historical Tancred did not seem to live up to Tancredi's status as a *chevalier sans peur et sans reproche*.[76] And as Tasso's popularity outside of Italy sharply decreased after World War I, and the remembrance of Tancred's heroic image faded, reassessments of his life in scholarship and fiction took a sharp change for the worse.[77] Nicholson's 1940 biography, still the last study dedicated entirely to Tancred, highlighted disapprovingly his troublesome role in the early history of the Kingdom of Jerusalem; and Runciman's extremely influential 1951 history of the crusades took this much further.[78] To Runciman, Tancred was a despicable character; he described Tancred as bleakly opportunistic, an arrogant man, 'distrusted and disliked', declaring (wrongly) that at his death 'the chroniclers could find few scenes of grief to report'.[79]

Despite its problematic sources, however, Runciman's evaluation has proven enduring: Thomas acknowledged him and Albert of Aachen as his chief historical sources, contextualising his extremely negative depiction of Tancred within these portrayals of him.[80] While Runciman indicted Tancred's moral character in the name of highlighting a supposedly better idea of crusader embodied, for instance, by Godfrey of Bouillon, as part of a layered relationship with the crusader movement in its entirety, Thomas's novel makes him the most despicable representative of a wholesale vicious army and ideal.[81] This tension, and that between the depictions of Tancred in Thomas's main sources, is emblematic: in it we can identify the final key to both the raising of the character of Tancred and his downfall through time.

The view of Tancred as a young, sometimes rash but ultimately effective 'holy warrior' has remained constant: his image as a young, short-tempered, militarily able crusader has not changed, even if he has become a secondary character in fiction, as writers have focused on his younger years. What has changed has been, substantially, the view of the movement he so successfully aided. When Runciman demonises Tancred to the point of ignoring the praise his contemporaries lavished on him, he is seizing on him as the knot of his discomfort with the idea of crusade itself: at once the host of charismatic and to him praiseworthy characters such as Godfrey of Bouillon and Bohemond, and 'a sin against the Holy Ghost'.[82] Discomfort with Tancred's self-evident success as a warrior on Christendom's frontier becomes emblematic of the discomfort with crusading as a whole. In this, Runciman functions as a link between two views of the crusade: a praiseworthy struggle for Christianity on the one hand, as depicted by Albert of Aachen, or the representation of all that is to be condemned about it, as done by Thomas. The transition of Tancred's character from 'perfect knight' to terrifying villain becomes emblematic of the transition of the crusade from cherished memory to dire warning.

In an entirely coherent way, for Albert of Aachen and Thomas both, Tancred is a ruthless standard-bearer and wager of holy war, but their different evaluations of him, ultimately, hinge on something not dependent on Tancred himself: the perception of the value or horror of the crusader enterprise as a whole. While Albert of Aachen saw in Tancred a praiseworthy defender, however flawed, of what he considered to be the ultimate good of Christian rule in Jerusalem, Thomas capitalised on Tancred's ferocity, exaggerating it, as a perfect emblem of its contrary. As a disturbingly young, terribly angry, and very violent crusader, Tancred became the ideal symbol to break with the romanticisation of the idea of crusade. The unmaking of Tancred's heroic depiction, then, helps us chart the fall of the idea of crusade, and effectively embodies the growing disenchantment with the first historical iteration of Christian holy war.

Notes

1 I wish to acknowledge the contribution of the Leverhulme Trust, as this chapter was written out of the research undertaken as the holder of a postdoctoral Leverhulme Study Abroad Studentship at the Università di Roma Tor Vergata, Rome, Italy (2018–19). I would like to thank Mike Horswell for his in-depth feedback and invitation to take part in this volume and Kristin Skottki for her very useful editing. All translations from Italian, Latin, and Greek are my own.
2 Edward Gibbon, *The History of the Decline and Fall of the Roman Empire*, vol. 3 (London: 1788), p. 53.
3 David C. Douglas, *The Norman Fate, 1100–1154* (London: 1976), p. 172.
4 Heinrich Hagenmeyer, ed., *Fulcheri Carnotensis Historia Hierosolymitana (1095–1127)*, (Heidelberg, 1913), p. 562, n.2; Francesca Petrizzo, 'The Ancestry and Kinship of Tancred, Prince Regent of Antioch', *Medieval Prosopography* 34 (2019), pp. 46–8.
5 The standard life of Tancred is Robert L. Nicholson, *Tancred* (Chicago, 1940). For his complex relationship with Bohemond see Francesca Petrizzo, '"Although He Was His Nephew": A Study of Younger Hautevilles Either Side of the Sea', *The Haskins Society Journal* 30 (2018), pp. 53–78 (forthcoming 2020).
6 Torquato Tasso, *Gerusalemme Liberata*, ed. Lanfranco Caretti (Turin, 2005), I.45.
7 Joseph François Michaud, *Histoire des croisades*, vol. 1 (Paris, 1812), for instance pp. 249, 478, 516.
8 Bernhard Kugler, *Boemund und Tankred, Fürsten von Antiochen* (Tübingen, 1862); Ralph B. Yewdale, *Bohemond I, Prince of Antioch* (Princeton, 1917), pp. 90, 100, 131; Claude Cahen, *La Syrie du Nord à l'époque des croisades et la principauté franque d'Antioche* (Paris, 1940); Tom Asbridge, *The Creation of the Principality of Antioch (1098–1130)* (Woodbridge 2000), pp. 53–60.
9 Nicholson, *Tancred*; Runciman, *Crusades*, 3 vols.
10 Simon John, *Godfrey of Bouillon* (London, 2018), p. 56; Jean Flori, *Bohémond d'Antioche* (Paris, 2007), p. 27; Susan B. Edgington, *Baldwin I of Jerusalem* (London, 2019), p. 1.
11 *The Deeds of the Franks*, ed. and trans. Rosalind Hill (Oxford, 1962), II.v, pp. 10–11.
12 Ibid., X.xxxv, pp. 84–7.

13 Ralph of Caen, *Tancredus*, ed. Edoardo d'Angelo (Turnhout, 2011), lines 17–20, p. 6.
14 *Albert of Aachen's History*, ed. and trans. Susan B. Edgington (Oxford, 2007), II.22, pp. 94–5.
15 Guibert de Nogent, *Dei gesta per Francos et cinq autres textes*, ed. R.B.C. Huygens (Turnhout, 1996), lines 763–5, p. 194.
16 *La Chanson d'Antioche*, ed. Suzanne Duparc-Quioc (Paris, 1976); *La Chanson de Jérusalem*, ed. Nigel R. Thorp (Tuscaloosa, 1992).
17 Torquato Tasso, *Lettere*, ed. Cesare Guasti (Florence, 1854), p. 60, n. 47.
18 Vincenzo Vivaldi, *Prolegomeni ad uno studio completo sulle fonti della Gerusalemme liberata* (Trani, 1904), pp. 85–7, 120–2; Michael Murrin, *History and Warfare in Renaissance Epic* (Chicago, 1994), pp. 112–14.
19 Franco Cardini, 'Torquato Tasso e la crociata' in *Torquato Tasso e la cultura estense*, ed. Gianni Venturi, vol. 2 (Florence, 1999), pp. 615–24, p. 621. See also Luigi Russo, 'Re-inventare la crociata nel Quattrocento. Il *De bello* di Benedetto Accolti' in *Quei maledetti Normanni*, eds. Jean-Marie Martin and Rosanna Alaggio, vol. 2 (Ariano Irpino-Naples, 2016), pp. 1039–54.
20 Phyllis Gaffney, *Constructions of Childhood and Youth in Old French Narrative* (Farnham, 2011), pp. 179–96; Francesco Sberlati, *Il genere e la disputa. La poetica fra Ariosto e Tasso* (Rome, 2002); Torquato Tasso, *Discorsi dell'arte poetica e del poema eroico*, ed. Luigi Poma (Bari, 1964).
21 Tasso, *Liberata*, III.17; XIX.106–8, p. 13.
22 Tasso, *Liberata*, I.45, p. 58; XVIII.100–1.
23 Domenico Tintoretto, *Tancred Baptising Clorinda* (1586–1600); Nicolas Poussin, *Tancred and Erminia* (1634); Pietro Ricchi, *Tancred and Erminia* (1660).
24 Voltaire, *Tancrède* (Paris, 1760).
25 Gioachino Rossini, *Tancredi* (1813, libretto by Gaetano Rossi).
26 Owen Jander, J.B. Steane, and Elizabeth Forbes, 'Contralto' in *The New Grove Dictionary of Opera*, ed. Stanley Sadie, vol. 1 (London, 1992), pp. 933–5.
27 Benjamin Disraeli, *Tancred: or, The New Crusade* (London, 1847).
28 The series is published under the pseudonym 'Jack Ludlow': *Son of Blood* (London, 2013); *Soldier of Crusade* (London, 2013); *Prince of Legend* (London, 2014). *Son of Blood*, pp. 382, 294–5; *Soldier of Crusade*, pp. 15–17.
29 Thomas Asbridge, *The First Crusade: A New History* (Oxford, 2004), p. 61.
30 Sini Kangas, 'Growing Up to Be a Crusader: The Next Generation' in *Jerusalem the Golden*, eds. Susan B. Edgington and Luis García-Guijarro (Turnhout, 2014), pp. 255–72.
31 *Tancredus*, 4387–95.
32 Ascanio Grandi, *Tancredi* (Lecce, 1868), 4.xcix; Daniela Foltran, *Per un ciclo tassiano. Imitazione, invenzione e 'correzione' in quattro proposte epiche fra Cinque e Seicento* (Alessandria, 2005), pp. 133–8.
33 Grandi, *Tancredi*, p. 10. Foltran, *Per un ciclo tassiano*, p. 184.
34 Giuseppe Tomasi di Lampedusa, *Il Gattopardo* (Milan, 1958), pp. 35, 42–4, 117–18, 120–1, 135–48.
35 Laverne Gay, *Wine of Satan* (New York, 1949).
36 Gay, *Wine of Satan*, pp. 104, 174, 270.
37 Alfred Duggan, *Count Bohemond* (London, 1964), p. 61.
38 Ibid., pp. 92–4, 127–9.
39 The books are published under the pseudonym 'Tom Harper': *The Mosaic of Shadows* (London, 2003); *Knights of the Cross* (London, 2006); *Siege of Heaven* (London, 2007).

Making and unmaking Tancred   21

40 See for instance Thomas, *Siege of Heaven*, pp. 570–600, for the massacre in Jerusalem.
41 Thomas, *Knights of the Cross*, pp. 118, 137–8; *Siege of Heaven*, pp. 67–8.
42 *The Deeds of the Franks*, X.xxxviii, p. 92.
43 *Annae Comnenae Alexias*, eds. Diether R. Reinsch and Athanasios Kambylis, Part I (Berlin, 2001), XI.iii.2, pp. 329–30.
44 Ibid., XIII.x, pp. 411–12.
45 *Tancredus*, lines 582–633, pp. 22–3.
46 Ibid., lines 555–600, pp. 21–2; 3784–5, p. 114.
47 Omero, *Iliade* (Turin, 2014), I, lines 53–305.
48 *Liberata*, V.32–49.
49 Ibid., I.46–8.
50 Ibid., IV.37–8; VI.27–30.
51 Ibid., VI.112–14; VII.
52 Ibid., XII.75–90.
53 Ibid., XIII.35, pp. 41–5.
54 Ibid., XVIII.100–1; XIX.114, 119; XX.83–5.
55 Marion Wells, *The Secret Wound* (Palo Alto, 2007), pp. 137–8.
56 Ibid., I.46; XVI.1 63.
57 On Tasso's fortune, see Elizabeth Siberry, 'Tasso and the Crusades: History of a Legacy', *Journal of Medieval History*, 19 (1993), pp. 163–9; *Tasso e l'Europa*, ed. Daniele Rota (Viareggio-Lucca, 1996).
58 *Annae Comnenae Alexias*, XII.ii.5, p. 363.
59 Albert of Aachen, *History*, xii.9, p. 836.
60 *Tancredus*, lines 1641–82, pp. 51–2.
61 Albert of Aachen, *History*, xii.8, p. 386.
62 Fulcher, *Historia*, II.xlvi, pp. 562–3.
63 In his translators' words, 'William's critical faculties cease to function when he writes of Tancred' (William of Tyre, *A History of Deeds Done Beyond the Sea*, trans. and ann. Emily A. Babcock and August C. Krey (New York, 1943), p. 186, n. 24).
64 Ibn al-Qalanisi, *The Damascus Chronicle of the Crusades*, trans. by R.A. Gibb (Mineola, 1932), pp. 90, 99; Ibn al-Athir, *The Chronicle of Ibn al-Athīr for the Crusading Period from al-Kāmil fī'l-ta'rīkh, Part I*, trans. Donald S. Richards (Farnham, 2007), pp. 92, 138–9, 141, 160.
65 Usama Ibn Munqidh, *The Book of Contemplation*, trans. Paul M. Cobb (London, 2008), pp. 77–9.
66 Peter Tudebode, *Historia de Hierosolymitano Itinere*, eds. and trans. John and Laurita Hill (Philadelphia, 1974), XI, p. 120.
67 *The Deeds of the Franks*, I.iiii, pp. 8–9; II.v, p. 11.
68 Asbridge, *Antioch*, pp. 53–60.
69 *Liberata*, V.32–8; XVIII.45–55; XIX.80–119 for Vafrino.
70 Gay, *Wine of Satan*, p. 297.
71 Duggan, *Count Bohemond*, pp. 280–1. Much like Gay, Duggan does not describe Tancred's independent rule: according to Evelyn Waugh, he had 'planned, but not committed to writing a novel about Tancred', which still seems to stress that, for the author, Tancred was a far less fascinating subject that his uncle (Evelyn Waugh, 'Preface' in *Count Bohemond*, p. 5).
72 Donachie, *Soldier of Crusade*, p. 114.
73 Thomas, *Knights of the Cross*, pp. 130–1; *Siege of Heaven*, pp. 67–8.

74 Kugler, *Boemund und Tankred* (1862); Yewdale, *Bohemond I* (1917); Cahen, *La Syrie du Nord* (1940).
75 Michaud, *Histoire des croisades*, vol. 1, pp. 249, 478, 516.
76 Salvatore Multineddu, *Le fonti della Gerusalemme liberata* (Turin, 1895), pp. 204–5.
77 For the heyday and decline of Tasso's popularity in England, see Jason Lawrence, *Tasso's Art and Afterlives* (Manchester, 2017).
78 Nicholson, *Tancred*, pp. 227–9; Runciman, *Crusades*.
79 Runciman, *Crusades*, 2, pp. 55, 126.
80 Thomas, *Knights of the Cross*, p. 447.
81 Runciman, *Crusades*, 1, pp. 146–7.
82 Ibid., 3, p. 480; 1, p. 57.

Bibliography

Primary

Albert of Aachen's History. Ed. and trans. Susan B. Edgington. Oxford: Clarendon Press 2007.
Annae Comnenae Alexias, Part I. Eds. Diether R. Reinsch and Athanasios Kambylis. Berlin: De Gruyter, 2001.
La Chanson d'Antioche. Ed. Suzanne Duparc-Quioc. Paris: Paul Geuthner, 1976.
La Chanson de Jérusalem. Ed. Nigel R. Thorp. Tuscaloosa, AL: University of Alabama Press, 1992.
The Deeds of the Franks. Ed. and trans. Rosalind Hill. Oxford: Clarendon Press, 1962.
Disraeli, Benjamin. *Tancred: or, The New Crusade*. London: Henry Colburn, 1847.
Duggan, Alfred. *Count Bohemond*. London: Faber & Faber, 1964.
Fulcheri Carnotensis Historia Hierosolymitana (1095–1127). Ed. Heinrich Hagenmeyer. Heidelberg: Carl Winters, 1913.
Gay, Laverne. *Wine of Satan: A Tale of Bohemond, Prince of Antioch*. New York: Scribner, 1949.
Gibbon, Edward. *The History of the Decline and Fall of the Roman Empire*. Vol. 3. London, 1788.
Grandi, Ascanio. *Tancredi*. Lecce: Tipografia Editrice Salentina, 1868.
Guibert de Nogent. *Dei gesta per Francos et cinq autres textes*. Ed. R.B.C. Huygens. Turnhout: Brepols, 1996.
Guillaume de Tyr. *Chronique*. Ed. R.B.C. Huygens. Turnhout: Brepols, 1986.
Harper, Tom [Edwin Thomas]. *The Mosaic of Shadows*. London: Arrow Books, 2003.
———. *Knights of the Cross*. London: Arrow Books, 2006.
———. *Siege of Heaven*. London: Arrow Books, 2007.
Ibn al-Athir. *The Chronicle of Ibn al-Athīr for the crusading period from al-Kāmil fī'l-ta'rīkh, Part I*. Trans. Donald S. Richards. Aldershot: Ashgate, 2007.
Ibn al-Qalanisi. *The Damascus Chronicle of the Crusades*. Trans. R.A. Gibb. Mineola: 1932.

Ludlow, Jack [David Donachie]. *Son of Blood*. London: Allison & Busby, 2012.
———. *Soldier of Crusade*. London: Allison & Busby, 2013.
———. *Prince of Legend*. London: Allison & Busby, 2014.
Omero, *Iliade*. Turin: Einaudi, 2014.
Peter Tudebode. *Historia de Hierosolymitano Itinere*. Eds. and trans. John and Laurita Hill. Philadelphia, PA: American Philosophical Society, 1974.
Ralph of Caen. *Tancredus*. Ed. Edoardo d'Angelo. Turnhout: Brepols, 2011.
Rossini, Gioachino. *Tancredi*(libretto by Gaetano Rossi). First represented Venice, 1813.
Tasso, Torquato. *Discorsi dell'arte poetica e del poema eroico*. Ed. Luigi Poma. Bari: Laterza, 1964.
———. *Gerusalemme Liberata*. Ed. Lanfranco Caretti. Turin: Einaudi, 2005.
———. *Lettere*. Ed. Cesare Guasti. Florence: Le Monnier, 1854.
Tomasi di Lampedusa, Giuseppe. *Il Gattopardo*. Milan: Mondadori, 1958.
Usama Ibn Munqidh. *The Book of Contemplation: Islam and the Crusades*. Trans. Paul M. Cobb. London: Penguin, 2008.
Voltaire. *Tancrède*. Paris: Prault, 1760.
William of Tyre. *A History of Deeds Done Beyond the Sea*. Trans. and annotated Emily A. Babcock and August C. Krey. New York: Octagon Books, 1976.

Secondary

Asbridge, Thomas. *The Creation of the Principality of Antioch (1098–1130)*. Woodbridge: Boydell, 2000.
———. *The First Crusade: A New History*. London: Free Press, 2004.
Cahen, Claude. *La Syrie du Nord à l'époque des croisades et la principauté franque d'Antioche*. Paris: IFPO, 1940.
Cardini, Franco. 'Torquato Tasso e la crociata'. In *Torquato Tasso e la cultura estense*. ed. Gianni Venturi. 3 vols. Florence: Leo S. Olschki, 1999, pp. 615–24.
Douglas, David C. *The Norman Fate, 1100–1154*. London: Eyre Methuen, 1976.
Edgington, Susan B. *Baldwin I of Jerusalem*. London: Routledge, 2019.
Flori, Jean. *Bohémond d'Antioche*. Paris: Payot, 2007.
Foltran, Daniela. *Per un ciclo tassiano. Imitazione, invenzione e 'correzione' in quattro proposte epiche fra Cinque e Seicento*. Alessandria: Edizioni dell'Orso, 2005.
Gaffney, Phyllis. *Constructions of Childhood and Youth in Old French Narrative*. Farnham: Ashgate, 2011.
Jander, Owen, J.B. Steane and Elizabeth Forbes. 'Contralto'. In *The New Grove Dictionary of Opera, Volume One: A–D*. ed. Stanley Sadie. London: Macmillan Reference, 1992, pp. 933–5.
John, Simon. *Godfrey of Bouillon*. London: Routledge, 2018.
Kangas, Sini. 'Growing Up to Be a Crusader: The Next Generation'. In *Jerusalem the Golden: The Origins and Impact of the First Crusade*. eds. Susan B. Edgington and Luis García-Guijarro. Turnhout: Brepols, 2014, pp. 255–72.
Kugler, Bernhard. *Boemund und Tankred, Fürsten von Antiochen*. Tübingen: Ludwig Friedrich Fues, 1862.

Lawrence, Jason. *Tasso's Art and Afterlives: The Gerusalemme Liberata in England*. Manchester: MUP, 2017.

Michaud, Joseph François. *Histoire des croisades*. Vol. 1. Paris: Furne, Jouvet & Delagrave, 1812.

Multineddu, Salvatore. *Le fonti della Gerusalemme liberata*. Turin: Carlo Clausen, 1895.

Murrin, Michael. *History and Warfare in Renaissance Epic*. Chicago, IL: University of Chicago Press, 1994.

Nicholson, Robert L. *Tancred: A Study of His Career and Work*. Chicago, IL: University of Chicago Press, 1940.

Petrizzo, Francesca. '"Although He Was His Nephew": A Study of Younger Hautevilles Either Side of the Sea'. *The Haskins Society Journal* 30 (2018), pp. 53–78. 2020.

———. 'The Ancestry and Kinship of Tancred, Prince Regent of Antioch'. *Medieval Prosopography* 34 (2019), pp. 41–83.

Rota, Daniele, ed. *Tasso e l'Europa. Atti del Convegno Internazionale. Università di Bergamo, 24-25-26 Maggio 1995*. Viareggio-Lucca: Mauro Baroni, 1996.

Runciman, Steven. *A History of the Crusades*. 3 Vols. Cambridge: CUP, 1951–4.

Russo, Luigi. *Boemondo. Figlio del Guiscardo e principe di Antiochia*. Avellino: E. Sellino, 2009.

———. 'Re-inventare la crociata nel Quattrocento. *Il De bello* di Benedetto Accolti'. In *'Quei maledetti Normanni': Studi offerti a Errico Cuozzo*. eds. Jean-Marie Martin and Rosanna Alaggio. 2 vols. Ariano Irpino-Naples: Centro Europeo di Studi Normanni. 2016, pp. 1039–54.

Sberlati, Francesco. *Il genere e la disputa. La poetica fra Ariosto e Tasso*. Rome: Bulzoni Editore, 2002.

Siberry, Elizabeth. 'Tasso and the Crusades: History of a Legacy'. *Journal of Medieval History* 19 (1993), pp. 163–9.

Vivaldi, Vincenzo. *Prolegomeni ad uno studio completo sulle fonti della Gerusalemme liberata*. Trani: V. Vecchi, 1904.

Wells, Marion. *The Secret Wound: Love Melancholy and Early Modern Romance*. Palo Alto, CA: Stanford University Press, 2007.

Yewdale, Ralph B. *Bohemond I, Prince of Antioch*. Princeton, NJ: Princeton University, 1917.

2 The memorialisation of Queen Melisende of Jerusalem
From the medieval to the modern

Danielle E.A. Park

Introduction: a forgotten queen?

The line between hero and villain can be a fine one; it hinges on the intentions and justification of actions, and is dependent on earlier constructions of past events.[1] Queen Melisende of Jerusalem (r. 1131–61), the first female ruler and heiress of the Kingdom of Jerusalem, is no exception. William of Tyre presented us with a paragon of queenship, while the French translation and continuation downplayed her role considerably – she was queen because her son lacked a wife, not because of her own claim. The continuation of Sigebert of Gembloux accused an anonymous queen of the murder of the Second Crusader Count Alphonse of Toulouse (the son of Count Raymond IV of Saint-Gilles, the First Crusader and founder of the county of Tripoli); William of Nangis was convinced of Melisende's guilt. In a relatively rare Early Modern appearance Melisende is described as Baldwin III's mother and 'partner with him in the kingdome'. In the twentieth century, Hans Eberhard Mayer believed 'her thirst for power was greater than her wisdom' and described how she 'spread her own tentacles toward Acre' to prevent Baldwin III (r. 1143–63) from establishing control in the north of the kingdom.[2]

Melisende is a significant figure for this volume for two key reasons. First, she is the only woman, and second, while well known to specialists, she looms less large in the popular consciousness than some of her contemporaries such as Eleanor of Aquitaine. As a case in point, Melisende is not mentioned in Celestia Bloss' *Heroines of the Crusades* (1854), while Eleanor represents the Second Crusade.[3] Since Melisende is a forgotten or at least unremembered hero in popular culture, her status as hero or villain is perhaps more subjective than that of the other figures included here. Scholarship has recognised her ambiguity: the heroism of a woman equalling her male crusader ancestors, alongside her potential casting as the villainous mother who jeopardised the kingdom by refusing to cede power to her own son, Baldwin III.⁴ As a woman who does not engage directly in warfare, she meets some but not all of the traditional criteria for a hero or a villain. This probably explains why there are comparatively few mentions of her in popular culture, and why she was largely side-lined in nineteenth-century histories which concentrated on male crusade protagonists, and defined Melisende by her relationships to men.⁵ Notable exceptions are the nineteenth-century pilgrimage accounts which remember Melisende as the patron of the churches and convent at Bethany.⁶

In light of her status as a largely forgotten figure, it is an understandable trend in popular writing to position Melisende as a figure to be (re)discovered, reclaimed, or rescued from the patriarchal and capricious historical record.⁷ The idea of this queen as 'untold women's history' is reflected in the synopsis for Kate Mosse's forthcoming (2022) play, *The Queen of Jerusalem*, which promises to celebrate 'the extraordinary woman who ruled Jerusalem in the 12th [*sic*] century'.⁸ From an academic perspective, the point is less that Melisende's history is untold than that it is not widely known to a mass audience; for example, a recent poster stated that 'Queen Melisende was a mere cipher'.⁹ From a marketing view, the idea that Melisende still needs to be brought to light adds a sense of mystery and discovery to the story of this woman.

Memory, or the lack thereof, is consequently one of the more prevalent themes in studies of this particular queen. This analysis extends even to the queen's burial place. Melisende's tomb was probably moved from the original burial chamber in the fourteenth century when the chapel was dedicated to the Virgin Mary's parents – Saint Ann and Saint Joachim. According to Prodomo, the Dominican Father Felix Faber was the last recorder of the location of Melisende's tomb at the end of the steps to the chapel in 1480.¹⁰ Part of Melisende's appeal lies in her gender and in the surviving material from her reign which can fit neatly into a proto-feminist narrative of a successful and intelligent woman in a man's world, equalling or bettering her male counterparts in ruling the frontier kingdom of Jerusalem.¹¹ Lines are drawn to relate and connect the medieval queen to the present to suggest a universal female experience.¹² The nature of the medieval source material leaves room for ambiguity, and in some cases invention, to fill the gaps and imagine the queen's daily life.¹³ This chapter will consider some of the popular accounts of Melisende. To determine the role of an authentic and authoritative framework, and conversely how much room there is for lively conjecture with a figure who is less well known to a wider audience, my principal lens is Judith Tarr's historical fiction *Queen of Swords* (1997). Tarr's work informs the majority of this chapter because of Melisende's absence in broader popular memories of the crusades. This makes Tarr's fleshed out portrayal much more significant and potentially influential, and as one of the few attempts to engage with Melisende in popular culture it merits a close investigation.

The celebrity historian and the queen of a golden age

The popularity and global influence of BBC-led historical accounts are well known.[14] Simon Sebag Montefiore's monograph *Jerusalem the Biography* and his 2012 television series *Jerusalem: The Making of a Holy City* highlighted Melisende's reign as a 'golden age' in the so-called Crusader States with the inclusion of a chapter describing her rule.[15] His perceived authority is a key element in both the text and its further influence: Lionsgate has plans for a character-driven *Game of Thrones*–style series, with Montefiore acting as both consultant and executive producer.[16]

Montefiore depicts Melisende as a cold individual in a frosty marriage in need of thawing. In common with Sir Steven Runciman – the influential Byzantine historian who authored the three-volume *A History of the Crusades* (1951–4) – he claims that 'if Melisende had lost her love, she had regained her power.'[17] The idea that Melisende could only choose between love and power is one we shall revisit in the historical fiction depiction of the queen. Montefiore gives some space to the building programme Melisende and her husband, Fulk of Anjou (r. 1131–43), undertook. He emphasises her long-term role in shaping Jerusalem, in the process making her directly relevant to the modern-day city the reader might be familiar with, and showing that her influence continues to be felt. Montefiore spends little time on the 'bittersweet moment' of Fulk's death and Melisende's and Baldwin III's succession. Likewise, he treats the civil war between Melisende and Baldwin III summarily. The nuances of the mother–son relationship after the queen stepped down are omitted. His final word on Melisende is 'the queen resigned power – and Jerusalem.' The point is less to analyse and more to narrate the key events in a diverting way within the wider narrative arc of the city of Jerusalem.[18] A similar approach informs one of the very few appearances of Melisende in fiction; *Queen of Swords* uses the key events of Melisende's life to inform the narrative of Tarr's fictional protagonists.

Queen of Swords: Melisende battles the Patriarchy

Historical fiction is one of the most accessible and influential genres of literary historicism. In light of this, it is possible to note generic developments of using lessons of the past from historical exemplars. Authors can draw lines between the past and present to show the continuities and shared experiences of the historical characters and the present reader. This is clear in the two historical fictions that incorporate Melisende. She does not feature as a character in *Lady Sibyl's Choice*, written in the nineteenth century for a young female audience. The novel represents a departure for nineteenth-century historical fiction focused on the crusades, featuring a female protagonist and narrator and concentrating on Melisende's granddaughter Queen Sibyl of Jerusalem's (d. 1160) decision to rule Jerusalem alongside her husband Guy de Lusignan (r. 1186–92) instead of choosing another nobleman to govern with her.[19] Melisende is in the historical appendix, where it is erroneously claimed that she predeceased Fulk of Anjou. This detail informs a plot device, which arguably speaks more to nineteenth-century concerns about female inheritance and autonomy than the medieval past that purportedly informs it. The narrator – the fictional Elaine, sister of Guy de Lusignan – laments the unfairness of Melisende's inheritance rights passing to her husband on their marriage and transferring to his family after her death.[20]

Melisende is featured much more prominently in the *Queen of Swords*.[21] With a PhD in Medieval Studies from Yale, Judith Tarr has authored more than 20 novels and her work is another departure from the norm of crusader-related fiction.[22] Female historical novels tend to subvert historical norms, while male historical fiction reinforces masculine values; Tarr gives us a romanticised queen – an ideal woman for the modern age. Tarr's Melisende is in charge; she is neither passive nor pliable, and she gives way only on her own terms. She speaks to gender and equality rather than masculine ideals of chivalry.[23] Tarr is interested in the values that her readers can relate to. Despite the title, Melisende is not the main protagonist of this novel, albeit that the chronology of the book follows Melisende's life cycle – first, lady and princess; second, queen regent; and third, queen mother. It is a key conceit of the novel that we observe Melisende only through the eyes of the protagonist Richildis – who becomes Melisende's lady-in-waiting and confidante – Richildis' brother Bertrand, or her nephew Arslan. Melisende is only part of the action when these characters are discussing her or are in her presence. This approach both adds intrigue to the plot and reaffirms the historical reality that we cannot know everything said behind closed doors. For example, a loaded conversation about Alice of Antioch's failed plot to control the regency of her young daughter Constance is left unfinished when the character Richildis withdraws and the veiled threat of Melisende's plan to take power in Jerusalem is left hanging.

> '[Alice] should also', said Melisende, 'have taught people to love her. She never thought of that, either.'
> 'The people love you' Hugh [of Jaffa] said, as if pondering it.
> Melisende smiled. 'They do', she said.
> 'Indeed, they do.'[24]

The memorialisation of Queen Melisende 29

De Groot notes the importance of perceived credibility, using the reviews of Philippa Gregory's historical fiction.[25] The sample size is smaller, but it is possible to conduct a similar exercise with Tarr's work, which potentially has more influence over how the reader engages with Melisende given the comparatively few mentions of her elsewhere. At the time of writing (December 2019), there are nine customer reviews of *Queen of Swords* on Amazon, and more than 150 ratings and 15 reviews on goodreads.com, alongside published reviews dating from the novel's publication in 1997. There are a few cases of overlap where the same review appears on both sites. In 2011, historical fiction author Elizabeth Chadwick ranked *Queen of Swords* as number 6 in her top 10 historical novels.[26] The novel has a bestseller ranking of 664,206 on amazon.co.uk and 2,329,463 on amazon.com.[27]

Realism, authenticity, and credibility are important to its reviewers. The contemporary reviews highlight that 'Tarr excels at bringing historical events to life', and comment on the focus on palace intrigue and the queen 'lusting for power'.[28] One Amazon reviewer comments on the entertaining story line 'always remaining true to historical events'.[29] Another reviewer notes that a sense of learned authority pervades the novel, which 'thrills like a thriller and teaches like a sophisticated faculty in medieval history'.[30] A goodreads.com reviewer comments that they were 'swept back to 12th century [*sic*] Jerusalem with all its sights and smells.'[31] The tension between historical accuracy and audience expectations is apparent here. The title *Queen of Swords* led at least one reviewer to assume that Melisende would take centre stage to a greater extent than the fictional protagonists.[32] These expectations of medieval heroism probably account for the lack of attention paid to Melisende in popular culture. It is not a coincidence that Melisende was first explored in any real depth in a novel written for a predominantly female audience by a woman. As Melisende was a queen who was not trained in weaponry, Tarr has to construct her in a different way from the conventional crusade hero. Instead, her focus is on the domestic and private sphere, and Melisende's weapon of choice is intrigue rather than the sword.

The reader engages indirectly with Runciman through the novel. A comparison of the main plot points shows that Tarr chose to adhere as far as possible to the 'facts' Runciman presented on Melisende. There is a clear attempt in the wedding scenes and their subsequent conversations – all of which are imagined for the novel – both to ensure that they ring true with Runciman's 'authoritative' version of the events and to enhance Tarr's credibility.[33] Tarr closely follows this portrayal of Melisende in her novel. Runciman asserted that Melisende had never cared for Fulk, 'despite his great love for her'.[34] This assessment underpins much of Tarr's novel. Her Fulk directly speaks of love in conversation with Count Hugh of Jaffa – the historical kinsman of Melisende who rebelled against Fulk in *c.* 1134. These romantic elements, however, do not detract from Fulk's attempts to rule as king in his own right in Tarr's version – a character trait that is observed in Melisende's and Fulk's first meeting.[35] Likewise, the manner in which the duel between Hugh and his stepson Walter plays out in the novel is almost identical to Runciman's depiction. Tarr even incorporated his speculations in her novelisation of these events that '[p]erhaps the Queen, alarmed that things had gone too far, begged [Hugh] to absent himself, or perhaps it was Countess Emma, appalled at the prospect of losing either husband or son.'[36] Details from Runciman such as the so-called 'oriental seclusion' that Raymond of Tripoli imposed on his wife – Melisende's sister Hodierna – by locking her in her chambers, and the questions of their daughter's legitimacy inform the queen's actions in Tarr's novel. The contrast between these two sisters is stark and Melisende is consistently her sister's superior: '"I would never have let myself be locked in at all," Melisende said.'[37]

Tarr's Melisende is an independent woman of both brains and beauty. The archaic language choice of 'nigh as fair' serves to set the scene and establish a 'medieval' aesthetic.[38] As well as establishing the family dynamic and her heritage, a short pen portrait sets Melisende up as a blond, headstrong princess prone to ignoring her maids and riding on horseback in the sun. She is an ideal princess for a modern audience. She is savvy and street-smart, but equally politically minded, calculating, and strategic. The first mention of her juxtaposes her and her father Baldwin II's gift-giving. The comparison is in Melisende's favour and underlines her insider status as a second-generation inhabitant of Outremer, whose Armenian mother Morphia 'had taught her to tell gold from dross, and deep-dyed silk from middling clever counterfeit'.[39] When the character Richildis first meets her, Melisende embodies elements of the 'poor, little rich girl' trope. Much like the contemporary Princess Jasmine from Disney's *Aladdin* of the 1990s, Tarr's Melisende rails against her lack of free choice in a husband, and more widely the threat that marriage poses to her independence and status. Later in the text, Tarr sets up the patriarchal socio-political context in which woman lack agency. Tarr's phrase '[t]hat was the lot of women in this world: to be disposed of as men saw fit' relates to Richildis.[40] However, the reader is equally invited to relate Melisende's experiences to this statement.

Tarr reveals the princess's intelligence and acumen to the reader through the activities of her ladies-in-waiting. The tasks Melisende sets them surprises Richildis, who comments on them sewing a robe of state and making lists for moving the court to Jerusalem for the wedding. The books read aloud to Melisende were 'not tales of old knights or lives of the saints, but the accounts of a great demesne'.[41] The effect of this on both the fictional Richildis and the reader is to give a very different impression of Melisende:

as a queen in waiting rather than a spoiled princess. Her independence and readiness for rule come across through her attention to detail and command of those around her. There is a sense of urgency and gendering of roles as the wedding approaches – Melisende's wedding preparations are likened to an army suddenly leaping into action after months of waiting. Tarr uses this scene to foreshadow both Melisende's talents as a potential ruler, her independent spirit and expectations, and the trouble to come with this marriage. Tarr repeats the idea that Melisende had not chosen Fulk again here, and the reiteration that this is not a love match – or even an equal match – reinforces how ill-suited they appear to be at this stage. Part of Melisende's determination in the novel comes from her sense of justice and rank. Tarr is not strictly accurate in her claim that Melisende 'was royal born and far above this man who had been born a mere count'.[42] She was born the daughter of the count of Edessa; but the basic point that Tarr means to convey here is the difference in their status at the time of their marriage, and the injustice of Fulk's actions. It is clear that Tarr wants her readers to recognise that the couple come from very different worlds – Melisende compares the precarious nature of Jerusalem to the relative security of France.[43]

Tarr's Melisende does not seem to be interested in men beyond their political uses. She frequently refers to men as fools, cowards, and idiots. More significantly, in a rare deviation from Runciman's narrative – where Melisende is indifferent to Fulk and instead intimate with Hugh of Jaffa, provoking gossip and dividing the court – Tarr removes love almost entirely from Melisende's liaison with the count. The reader is left in no doubt regarding the sincerity of Hugh's feelings. It is explicit in the novel that Hugh loves the queen for herself and not her crown (unlike the depiction of Fulk up until this point) and Melisende is aware of this. This changes nothing for Melisende; she swears Hugh will never have her.[44] Tarr inverts Runciman's assertion that Melisende consoled herself with power when thwarted in love. It becomes clear that in Tarr's characterisation Melisende is motivated by, and thrives on, power and little else. To that end her piety is hinted at being a political prop to keep her on the throne as she grows older – and a potential source of her return to power after her stepping down in favour of Baldwin. This use of the Church is another detail that informed part of Runciman's argument. The chronology of Melisende's and Baldwin III's civil war also adheres closely to Runciman's narrative.[45]

Power informs most of Melisende's actions and even underpins her appearance. Tarr emphasises Melisende's beauty repeatedly and stresses agelessness as one of her qualities despite the time jumps in the novel. While a few concessions are made to the passage of time, Tarr uses her beauty to show how at ease her Melisende is with power. She is so much in her element when in control of the kingdom that she defies time and becomes even more resplendent – an image underlined by the descriptions of her crown and gold clothing that highlight her royal status. She appears almost constantly clothed in gold until she steps down. Her wardrobe is tactical – a means of waging war with women's weapons; at the denouement, beside her plain widow's garb Baldwin appears 'almost gaudy'. It is only at the point that Melisende steps down that she is described as grey and touched with 'desiccating age'.[46] Her beauty is intertwined with the power she exerts and the loss of one impacts the other, an authorial device that further serves to win the audience to Melisende's side in the conflict with her son. The reader is invited to question why this woman had to step down, and to share in her implied triumph that Baldwin was forced to concede queenship to his mother within a few years of his victory. In this way, Melisende is an archetypal 'career' woman. We are given a clear insight into Melisende's character, and where she sees her role in Tarr's Jerusalem.[47]

Tarr portrays Melisende as conflicted between family and position, a context that was probably designed to chime with feminist concerns that their husbands wished to keep them barefoot, pregnant, and vulnerable.[48] Here she is an independent woman refusing to be defined by her relationships to husband and son. Her intention to limit the number of children – citing fears that her husband will side-line her by keeping her pregnant and 'ox-witted' – seems intended to make Melisende appeal to women in modern times.[49] The birth of Amalric, their second son, is treated as another part of Melisende's design. Despite the violence towards women depicted in the novel, there is no hint that Fulk forced Melisende to bear him another son. She is always in control.[50] Fulk's reaction to Baldwin's birth, however, is telling: 'her husband had barely acknowledged her existence, still less her part in the birthing of his son.' The use of 'his' reinforces Fulk's attempted erasure of his wife in this scene and the power struggle between these two – which now encompasses Baldwin.[51] Ownership of their son is part of her plan to mould him in her image. The focus on loyalty, legitimacy, and authority in terms of her claims to power is noteworthy and intended to ring true. In her right to choose and her bodily autonomy there is more artistic licence at play. Anachronism and authenticity inform in equal measure.

When Fulk accuses her of having an affair with Hugh of Jaffa, Tarr wants her readers to identify with Melisende and she ensures that her character imbues the virtues of a proto-feminist.[52] Melisende asks: 'And why may a man tup a whore on horseback, but a woman may not even kiss her friend on the cheek?'[53] The reader is invited to compare her dancing with Hugh to the revelation of Fulk's dalliance with a camp follower and appreciate the double standard. The argument is gradually revealed to be about more than Hugh; it is about power, which Fulk eventually concedes to her after the fallout of her liaison. While Tarr does not present the queen as blameless, it is clear that Fulk is more culpable for withholding power from her. Tarr presents a similar situation later in the novel. When Melisende has approved breaking faith with Damascus, the character Bertrand notes another double standard that they hold the queen to, in turn inviting the reader to question the fairness of the verdict.[54] The gender and status inequality is stark and speaks to the 1990s audience – an experienced woman set against a younger man. Richildis makes a similar observation about Melisende and Eleanor of Aquitaine as queens: 'Odd: neither wants to be a man. Simply, to have what a man has.'[55] In this regard, Tarr's Melisende is a woman out of step with time; it later falls to Richildis to explain why the queen cannot rule alone as a woman: 'no man can forget the plain fact of your sex. No man ever will.'[56]

Melisende retains a spark of defiance and free will.[57] Tarr is keen to impress on her readers that the queen surrenders only on her own terms, not simply because she is a woman in a man's world. Richildis' observations are the last time we see Melisende directly in the novel, and they serve to underscore the incompleteness of Baldwin's victory – he has won only because his mother has allowed it, and it is not a lasting defeat.[58] In remarkable contrast to this, the final mentions of the queen in the novel show that, for now at least, her status is diminished. Melisende's name stands for wilful ignorance, impotence, and failing to recognise another's status. She is invoked in two conversations; the first between Arslan – who wishes to take charge of the fictional family estate in France – and Richildis who exclaims, 'I am not Melisende' to recognise Arslan's new position. The second takes place as Bertrand reflects on his own and his son's new standing: 'As the queen belongs in Nablus? Shall I be so impotent, then?' Despite the ridicule here, the author's note serves as an epilogue to recount Melisende's return to power.[59]

A flawed but feminist hero

One frequent note of Melisende's character is the lack of emotion she displays. The relationship between mother and son is strained in the novel, even before Baldwin presses his claims to the throne more seriously.[60] Tarr chooses to have the boy look on his mother with awe rather than affection – perhaps the price of her earlier indifference and recognition that Melisende cannot 'have it all'. Later in the novel, Baldwin wishes she would be more of a 'natural mother' and step down in his favour – implying that she has chosen power over love once again. As Baldwin II lies dying, Tarr's version of Melisende is a brisk woman lacking tenderness. She refuses to allow excessive weeping and mourning in her father's presence. When Fulk leaves her in command of Jerusalem after Hugh of Jaffa's alliance with Ascalon, she comes across as a level-headed ruler, not rash enough to jeopardise her victory by following her husband against his wishes.[61]

Her emotions come to the fore only twice. After the attack on Hugh of Jaffa, Tarr tells us 'Melisende was in a white rage.'[62] In the novelisation of Fulk's death in a hunting accident, Melisende has far greater agency and influence. The escapade is referred to as the 'queen's hunt', and a contest between husband and wife ensues at her instigation. She is much more central to the king's death in this scene; Fulk spurs his horse and gives it its head to catch up with the queen, who rides a horse-length ahead. The hare that is so significant in William of Tyre's version is more incidental to the plot.[63] It is still startled from cover and causes the king's stallion to stagger and fall, but in Tarr's version the king is trying to catch the queen, not the hare. This detail underlines the nature of their relationship, which is made even starker by the uncharacteristic manner in which Melisende mourns him. The break with her usual character is clear.[64]

Much like the historical Melisende, Tarr's version has only so much time to grieve before she must take the reins of power. This moment represents the culmination of a plan hinted at when Baldwin was born, to rule alongside him. Tarr uses regency as a ploy for Melisende to claim power but leaves the reader in no doubt that she remains queen. Through the fictional Arslan we observe Melisende's face at this point: 'Its eyes were burning. Grief, yes, and pain, and guilt – whatever that was for. And a kind of white, fierce triumph. As if she had won something.'[65] Tarr brings the distinctions between sisters, this time Melisende and Alice, to the fore again as more of Melisende's careful and strategic planning comes to fruition. Tarr's language is telling in the image of Melisende she wants us to remember, a woman whose rightful place was as queen beside a king – either husband or son. It is her status that conveys the title king to her male relatives. Her superiority is clear in all the rites of the coronation in which Tarr describes the queen taking precedence.[66]

A running theme is her support of other women – most notably Hodierna and the protagonist Richildis. There is a sense of these women as allies, which again taps into the proto-feminism that underpins the narrative. When Richildis' brother seems set to refuse to allow her to marry the Byzantine Michael Bryennius, she invokes the queen, whom he cannot challenge.[67] Melisende later presents Richildis with a charter giving her – not her husband – ownership of an estate. Again, we see the queen as an astute gift-giver; the estate is within a day's ride of Jerusalem, keeping an ally close, and it contains a vineyard which harps back to Bertrand's and Richildis' family estate in France (this territory is a key plot point). The scene shows how much Melisende relishes her power and status in conveying this land where she wishes. Melisende's niece Constance represents a failing on the queen's part – she is unable to persuade her to remarry but the characterisation of the Antiochene princess demonstrates Melisende's greatest achievement – the legacy of sole female rule.[68]

Identity is another important theme in popular works; Melisende's mixed heritage from the Franks through her father's line and Armenia through Morphia is her saving grace on numerous occasions. As a second-generation ruler her accent, appearance, and policies are informed by her upbringing and familiarity with the East and its customs.[69] At one of her earliest meetings with Fulk, she orchestrates a display of the benefits of some co-operation with Muslims – in contrast to Fulk's men, who espouse the ideas of the crusade and consider adopting Eastern customs a threat to their Christian faith. Melisende's words and actions provide a direct challenge to this and set up the need for Fulk to rely on her advice more than he does: 'And for a fact, if donning a turban and drinking sherbet makes a man a Muslim, then he was never much of a Frank to begin with.'[70] At this moment servants arrive with pitchers of sherbet; Tarr leaves it ambiguous whether this was intended or not. The reader is presented with a woman who knows the practical realities of the political situation – where a male newcomer is promoted to king above her purely because of his gender, not his merit.[71] Tarr's Melisende speaks both to concerns about the agency of women in popular conceptions of medieval history and to the late 1990s concerns about the status of women in the work place. 'It was as if, to be a queen, a woman needed to be something other than woman; to be not a little like a man.'[72] Such a proto-feminist hero needs a fitting nemesis, and Tarr crafted Fulk to be a match for Melisende at this stage. Tarr's Fulk is aware of Melisende's intrigue and plans to take power. When Fulk goes to Antioch, his chancellors and seneschals rule in his stead, not his wife, who is forbidden from seeking power.[73]

After Fulk's death, the character's main conflict is with her son Baldwin. The Second Crusade forms the backdrop for much of this part of the novel. There is a distinct gap between the academic history and the public portrayal of the events when Melisende reacts to the loss of Edessa by asking for a crusade.[74] The fact that Melisende is able to recruit a crusade – there is no discussion of the crusaders' motivations beyond her appeal – is telling. This is particularly so in the context of the novel, where we are told this is the first crusade since 1095; the erroneous time gap only underlines her achievement. The Second Crusade and its aftermath reinforce both Melisende's limitations as well as her successes; it is during strategy meetings and the outcomes of military ventures that male characters first begin to voice concern at her influence and question her on the basis of her sex. Soldiers juxtapose their lack of water and deprivation while Melisende is not leading her armies but sitting in comfort.[75] Later in the novel, such men prove to be the turning point in Melisende's fortunes; they join Baldwin against her because they 'saw a woman, still beautiful but no longer young, who had never led an army, never fought with lance and sword in defence of the Holy Sepulchre'.[76] Significantly, Arslan is one of the earliest characters to refer to Melisende as 'queen mother', a lowering of her status that highlights his allegiance to Baldwin.[77] Melisende herself comments on the situation in the later stages of the novel. The focus on her legitimacy fits with the historical record but applies equally to the issue of female equality. In one of her final conversations with her son – at the height of their conflict – Melisende tears down the patriarchy's fragile excuse for why she cannot rule: 'God's law', said Melisende, 'is less than precise. There is nothing that ordains that a queen and heir must give way before a child whose only right resides in the fact of his sex.'[78]

Conclusion

Tarr's Melisende is to some extent a thwarted figure: an authoritative, formidable woman prevented by her gender from laying lasting claim to her birth right. She is a woman born and raised in all but one way – the art of war – to be king, but ultimately denied because she is female. Her reluctance and indeed resistance to accept her role as a mother and be defined by her relationships to men are themes that Tarr's late nineties and early noughties audiences would recognise, and possibly relate to in the context of concerns that pregnancy and childcare could hold a woman back from her career. Portraying Melisende in this way makes her experience as a woman, if not as a queen, more universal and relevant to Tarr's own period. Tarr does not stray too far from her source material (William of Tyre via Runciman), but the more overt proto-feminist claims on child birth and her autonomy over her body speak as much – if not more – to the time they were written in than to the twelfth-century setting. That being said, there is clear need to impress a sense of credibility on this version of Melisende through the focus on her legitimacy, prudence, and right to rule – albeit with a 1990s spin on the medieval social context that Tarr reconfigures as a quest for gender equality. Popular historical approaches to Melisende take a similar line and embrace the queen as a proto-feminist figurehead and view her and accounts of her through a feminist lens. But for all these credentials as a proto-feminist hero who ruled in a 'golden age', she is also a figure who needs rescuing. Notably this defence is not against the claims of her near contemporaries – which we have seen include accusations of poisoning Alphonse of Toulouse – but from more modern patriarchal history that some popular historians claim has side-lined her far more effectively than Fulk and Baldwin III ever could.[79]

Notes

1 For example, Geoffrey Cubitt, *History and Memory* (Manchester, 2007), pp. 56, 214.
2 William of Tyre, *Chronicon, Corpus Christianorum, Continuatio Mediaevalis*. vol. 63A. ed. Robert B.C. Huygens (Turnhout, 1986), p. 777; *Guillaume de Tyr et ses continuateurs* 2, ed. M. Paulin Paris (Paris, 1879), p. 92; Sarah Lambert, 'Queen or Consort? Rulership and Politics in the Latin East, 1118–1228' in *Queens and Queenship in Medieval Europe*, ed. Anne J. Duggan (Woodbridge, 1997), pp. 153–69; Continuation of Sigebert of Gembloux, *Monumenta Germaniae Historica Scriptores 6* (Hannover, 1844), p. 454; William of Nangis, *Chronique latine de Guillaume de Nangis de 1113 à 1300*, ed. Hercule Géraud (Paris, 1843), 1, p. 43; Richard Knolles, *The Generall Historie of the Turkes* (London, 1603), p. 31; Hans Eberhard Mayer, 'Studies in the History of Queen Melisende', *Dumbarton Oaks Papers* 26 (1972), pp. 166, 130.
3 Celestia A. Bloss, *Heroines of the Crusades* (Aubern, 1854), pp. 264–98.
4 Peter Edbury and John G. Rowe, *William of Tyre* (Cambridge, 1988), p. 82.
5 For example, Leopold von Ranke, *Weltgeschichte* 4 (Leipzig, 1883), pp. 103, 134; Edmund Bohum, *A Geographical Dictionary* (London, 1688), p. 419; James T. Barclay, *The City of the Great King* (Philadelphia, 1858), p. 350; Charles Mills, *The History of the Crusades*, vol. 1 (London, 1820), p. 273.
6 For example, J. Krayenbelt, *Het Heilige Land* (Rotterdam, 1895), p. 91; William Henry Bartlett, *Footsteps of our Lord and His Apostles in Syria, Greece and Italy etc* (London, 1851), p. 163; John Price Durbin, *Observations in the East* (New York, 1847), p. 248.
7 Rosemary Mitchell, 'The Red Queen and the White Queen: Exemplification of Medieval Queens in Nineteenth-Century Britain' in *Heroic Reputations and Exemplary Lives*, eds. Geoffrey Cubitt and Allen Warren (Manchester, 2000), pp. 157–77; Margaret Tranovich, *Melisende of Jerusalem: The World of a Forgotten Crusader Queen* (London, 2011), pp. 17–18, 21, 25, 115, 117, 160, 164.
8 'Plays', *Kate Mosse website*, <https://web.archive.org/save/https://www.katemosse.co.uk/plays/>, [accessed 28 August 2019].
9 *Quora*, <www.quora.com/If-Matilda-of-Normandy-had-won-the-Anarchy-and-crowned-Queen-of-England-what-would-Geoffrey-of-Anjous-title-and-position-have-been>, [accessed 15 January 2020].
10 Tranovich, *Melisende*, pp. 13, 18, 117; Alberto Prodomo, 'The Tomb of Queen Melisenda', in *New Discoveries at the Tomb of Virgin Mary in Gethsemane*, eds. Bellarmino Bagatti, Michel Piccirillo, and Alberto Prodomo, trans. L. Sciberras (Jerusalem, 1975), p. 92.
11 Tranovich, *Melisende*, p. 18; Sharan Newman, *Defending the City of God* (New York, 2014), pp. 2, 179, 214–16, 218.
12 Diane F. Britton, 'Public History and Public Memory', *The Public Historian* 19 (1997), p. 14; Kathy Nawrot, 'Making Connections with Historical Fiction', *The Clearing House* 69 (1996), pp. 343–5; Grant Rodwell, *Whose History? Engaging History Students through Historical Fiction* (Adelaide, 2013), pp. 39, 44.
13 Tranovich, *Melisende*, pp. 14, 134–8, 161; Newman, *Defending*, p. 62.
14 Jerome De Groot, *Consuming History* (Abingdon, 2009), pp. 31, 154. See also Jerome De Groot, *The Historical Novel* (Abingdon, 2009).
15 Simon Sebag Montefiore, *Jerusalem* (London, 2011), pp. 264–77.

16 *Simon Sebag Montefiore website*, <https://web.archive.org/save/http://www.simonsebagmontefiore.com/jordan-attached-to-screenwrite-montefiores-jerusalem/>, [accessed 28 August 2019].
17 Sebag Montefiore, *Jerusalem*, p. 266.
18 Ibid., pp. 273, 279–82.
19 Megan L. Morris, 'Emily Sarah Holt's Lady Sybil's Choice: A Tale of the Crusades', *Crusades Project, University of Rochester*, <https://web.archive.org/web/20200220112137/https://d.lib.rochester.edu/crusades/text/lady-sybils-choice>, [accessed 19 January 2020].
20 Emily Sarah Holt, *Lady Sybil's Choice* (London, 1879), pp. 335, 249.
21 Judith Tarr, *Queen of Swords* (New York, 1997).
22 Joep Leerson, 'Literary Historicism: Romanticism, Philologists, and the Presence of the Past', *Modern Language Quarterly*, 65:2 (2004), p. 239; Lotte Jensen, 'Literature as Access to the Past: The Rise of Historical Genres in the Netherlands, 1800–1850' in *Free Access to the Past*, eds. Lotte Jensen, Joep Leerssen and Marita Mathijsen-Verkooijen (Leiden, 2010), pp. 130, 146; Siberry, *New Crusaders*, p. 149.
23 De Groot, *Historical Novel*, pp. 79–80.
24 Tarr, *Queen*, p. 136.
25 De Groot, *Consuming History*, p. 12.
26 'Queen of Swords', *goodreads.com*, <https://web.archive.org/web/20200220112823/https://www.goodreads.com/book/show/72849.Queen_of_Swords>, [accessed 20 February 2020]; 'Elizabeth Chadwick's top 10 historical novels', *Guardian.co.uk*, <https://web.archive.org/web/20200220113544/https://www.theguardian.com/books/top10s/top10/0,,1234234,00.html> [accessed 12 January 2019].
27 'Queen of Swords', *Amazon.co.uk*, <https://web.archive.org/save/https://www.amazon.co.uk/Queen-Swords-Judith-Tarr/dp/0312868057/ref=tmm_pap_swatch_0?_encoding=UTF8&qid=1579179604&sr=8-2>, [accessed 12 December 2019].
28 'Review of Queen of Swords', *Publishers Weekly* (April 1998), p. 66; 'Review of Queen of Swords', *Kirkus Reviews* (Dec 1997), p. 1764; 'Review of Queen of Swords', *Booklist* (June 1998), p. 822; 'Review of Queen of Swords', *Library Journal* (June 1998), p. 108.
29 'Queen of Swords, *Amazon.co.uk*.
30 Ibid.
31 'Queens of Swords', *goodreads.com*.
32 *Publishers Weekly*, p. 66.
33 Runciman, *Crusades*, 2, p. 178; Tarr, *Queen*, p. 464.
34 Ibid., p. 18; Runciman, *Crusades*, 2, p. 191.
35 Tarr, *Queen*, pp. 22, 147.
36 Runciman, *Crusades*, 2, p. 192; Tarr, *Queen*, p. 144.
37 Ibid., p. 408.
38 Ibid., p. 17.
39 Ibid., p. 16.
40 Ibid., p. 41.
41 Ibid., p. 42.
42 Ibid., pp. 43, 122.
43 Ibid., p. 44.
44 Ibid., pp. 146, 151, 218, 439, 443, 132, 143; Runciman, *Crusades*, 2, p. 191.

45 Ibid., 2, pp. 193, 231, 333; Tarr, *Queen*, pp. 153, 327, 393, 448.
46 Ibid., pp. 248, 327, 445, 443.
47 Ibid., p. 45.
48 Ibid., p. 67.
49 Ibid., p. 68.
50 Ibid., p. 164.
51 Ibid., p. 88.
52 Ibid., p. 132; Gabriele Griffin, 'Second Wave Feminism' in *A Dictionary of Gender Studies* (Oxford, 2017); Ian Buchanan, 'Second Wave Feminism' in *A Dictionary of Critical Theory*, 2nd ed. (Oxford, 2018).
53 Tarr, *Queen*, pp. 139–40.
54 Ibid., pp. 146, 245.
55 Ibid., p. 287.
56 Ibid., pp. 443–4.
57 Ibid., p. 444.
58 Ibid., pp. 445–7.
59 Ibid., pp. 453, 456, 463.
60 Ibid., p. 87.
61 Ibid., pp. 106, 251, 113, 116.
62 Ibid., pp. 150–1.
63 William of Tyre, *Chronicon*, p. 710.
64 Tarr, *Queen*, pp. 170–1, 178.
65 Ibid., pp. 180–1.
66 Ibid., pp. 182–4.
67 Ibid., pp. 196–7.
68 Ibid., pp. 201, 407.
69 For example, Newman, *Defending*, pp. 49, 79, 100, 143, 181.
70 Tarr, *Queen*, p. 52.
71 Ibid., pp. 52, 131.
72 Ibid., p. 165.
73 Ibid., p. 131.
74 Ibid., pp. 218–19.
75 Ibid., p. 250.
76 Ibid., pp. 439–40.
77 Ibid., p. 402.
78 Ibid., p. 433.
79 Tranovich, *Melisende*, pp. 13, 18, 117; Newman, *Defending*, p. 218.

Bibliography

Primary

Continuation of Sigebert of Gembloux. *Monumenta Germaniae Historica Scriptores 6*. Hannover: Hahn, 1844.

Barclay, James T. *The City of the Great King*. Philadelphia, PA: James Challen and Sons, 1858.

Bartlett, William Henry. *Footsteps of our Lord and His Apostles in Syria, Greece and Italy etc*. London: Arthur Hall, 1851.

Bloss, Celestia A. *Heroines of the Crusades*. Aubern: Alden, Beardsley and Co., 1854.

Bohum, Edmund. *A Geographical Dictionary*. London: Charles Brome, 1688.

Edbury, P. and John G Rowe. *William of Tyre: Historian of the Latin East*. Cambridge: CUP, 1988.

'Elizabeth Chadwick's top 10 historical novels', *Guardian.co.uk*, https://web.archive.org/web/20200220113544/https://www.theguardian.com/books/top10s/top10/0,1234234,00.html. [Accessed 12 January 2019].

Guillaume de Tyr et ses continuateurs. Ed. M. Paulin Paris. Vol. 2. Paris: Didot, 1879.

Holt, Emily Sarah. *Lady Sybil's Choice*. London: John F. Shaw and Company, 1879.

Knolles, Richard. *The Generall Historie of the Turkes*. London: Adam Islip, 1603.

Krayenbelt, J. *Het Heilige Land: Reis door Egypte, Palestina & Syrië*. Rotterdam: Wenk and Birkhoff, 1895.

Mayer, Hans Eberhard. 'Studies in the History of Queen Melisende'. *Dumbarton Oaks Papers* 26 (1972), pp. 93–182.

Mills, Charles. *The History of the Crusades for the Recovery and Possession of the Holy Land*. Vol. 1. London: Longman, 1820.

Newman, Sharan. *Defending the City of God: A Medieval Queen, the First Crusades, and the Quest for Peace in Jerusalem*. New York: Palgrave Macmillan, 2014.

'Plays'. *Kate Mosse Website*. https://web.archive.org/save/https://www.katemosse.co.uk/plays/. [Accessed 28 August 2019].

Price Durbin, John. *Observations in the East: Chiefly in Egypt, Palestine, Syria, and Asia Minor*. Vol. 1. New York: Harper and Brothers, 1847.

'Queen of Swords'. *Amazon.co.uk*. https://web.archive.org/save/https://www.amazon.co.uk/Queen-Swords-Judith-Tarr/dp/0312868057/ref=tmm_pap_swatch_0?_encoding=UTF8&qid=1579179604&sr=8-2. [Accessed 12 December 2019].

'Queen of Swords'. *goodreads.com*. https://web.archive.org/web/20200220112823/https://www.goodreads.com/book/show/72849.Queen_of_Swords. [Accessed 20 February 2020].

Quora, www.quora.com/If-Matilda-of-Normandy-had-won-the-Anarchy-and-crowned-Queen-of-England-what-would-Geoffrey-of-Anjous-title-and-position-have-been. [Accessed 15 January 2020].

von Ranke, Leopold. *Weltgeschichte*. Vol. 4. Leipzig: Duncker and Humblot, 1883.

'Review of 'Queen of Swords', *Booklist* (June 1998), p. 822.

'Review of Queen of Swords', *Kirkus Reviews* (December 1997), p. 1764.

'Review of 'Queen of Swords', *Library Journal* (June 1998), p. 108.

'Review of Queen of Swords', *Publishers Weekly* (April 1998), p. 66.

Sebag Montefiore, Simon. *Jerusalem: The Biography*. London: Weidenfeld and Nicolson, 2011.

Simon Sebag Montefiore Website. www.simonsebagmontefiore.com/jordan-attached-to-screenwrite-montefiores-jerusalem/. [Accessed 28 August 2019].

Tarr, Judith. *Queen of Swords*. New York: Forge, 1997.

Tranovich, Margaret. *Melisende of Jerusalem: The World of a Forgotten Crusader Queen*. London: East and West Publishing, 2011.

William of Nangis. *Chronique latine de Guillaume de Nangis de 1113 à 1300*. Ed. Hercule Géraud. Vol. 1. Paris: Chez Jules Renouard, 1843.

William of Tyre. *Chronicon. Corpus Christianorum, Continuatio Mediaevalis*. Ed. Robert B.C. Huygens. Vol. 63A. Turnhout: Brepols, 1986.

Secondary

Britton, Diane F. 'Public History and Public Memory'. *The Public Historian* 19 (1997), pp. 11–23.
Buchanan, Ian. 'Second Wave Feminism'. In *A Dictionary of Critical Theory*. 2nd ed. Oxford: OUP, 2018.
Cubitt, Geoffrey. *History and Memory*. Manchester: MUP, 2007.
De Groot, Jerome. *Consuming History: Historians and Heritage in Contemporary Popular Culture*. Abingdon: Routledge, 2009.
———. *The Historical Novel*. London: Routledge, 2009.
Griffin, Gabriele. 'Second Wave Feminism'. In *A Dictionary of Gender Studies*. Oxford: OUP, 2017.
Jensen, Lotte. 'Literature as Access to the Past: The Rise of Historical Genres in the Netherlands, 1800–1850'. In *Free Access to the Past: Romanticism, Cultural Heritage and the Nation*. eds. Lotte Jensen, Joep Leerssen and Marita Mathijsen-Verkooijen. Leiden: Brill, 2010, pp. 127–46.
Lambert, Sarah. 'Queen or Consort? Rulership and Politics in the Latin East, 1118–1228'. In *Queens and Queenship in Medieval Europe: Proceedings of a Conference Held at Kings College London, April 1995*. ed. Anne J. Duggan. Woodbridge: Boydell Press, 1997, pp. 153–69.
Leerson, Joep. 'Literary Historicism: Romanticism, Philologists, and the Presence of the Past'. *Modern Language Quarterly* 65:2 (2004), pp. 221–43.
Mitchell, Rosemary. 'The Red Queen and the White Queen: Exemplification of Medieval Queens in Nineteenth-Century Britain'. In *Heroic Reputations and Exemplary Lives*. eds. Geoffrey Cubitt and Allen Warren. Manchester: MUP, 2000, pp. 157–77.
Morris, Megan L. 'Emily Sarah Holt's Lady Sybil's Choice: A Tale of the Crusades', *Crusades Project, University of Rochester*. https://web.archive.org/web/20200220112137/https://d.lib.rochester.edu/crusades/text/lady-sybils-choice. [Accessed 19 January 2020].
Nawrot, Kathy. 'Making Connections with Historical Fiction'. *The Clearing House* 69 (1996), pp. 343–45.
Prodomo, Alberto. 'The Tomb of Queen Melisenda'. In *New Discoveries at the Tomb of Virgin Mary in Gethsemane*. eds. Bellarmino Bagatti, Michel Piccirillo, and Alberto Prodomo. Trans. L. Sciberras. Jerusalem: Franciscan Printing Press, 1975.
Rodwell, Grant. *Whose History? Engaging History Students through Historical Fiction*. Adelaide: University of Adelaide Press, 2013.
Runciman, Steven. *A History of the Crusades: Volume 2, The Kingdom of Jerusalem and the Frankish East, 1100–1187*. Cambridge: CUP, 1952.
Siberry, Elizabeth. *The New Crusaders: Images of the Crusades in the Nineteenth and Early Twentieth Centuries*. Aldershot: Ashgate, 2000.

3 Oppressor, martyr, and Hollywood villain

Reynald of Châtillon and the representation of crusading violence

John D. Cotts

After the battle of Hattin in 1187, the Ayyubid Sultan Saladin personally executed Reynald of Châtillon, lord of Transjordan and formerly prince of Antioch. Contemporary chroniclers writing in several languages agree on that point. For the past nine centuries, however, Reynald's life and death have inspired widely divergent interpretations in histories, novels, and even cinema and sculpture. Saladin's biographer Baha' al-Din Ibn Shaddad (d. 1234), who vividly recounted the death scene, called Reynald a 'monstrous infidel and terrible oppressor', and so summarised the overwhelming consensus of Arabic writers as to his character.[1] After all, Reynald had broken truces with Saladin and attacked peaceful caravans, and some observers thought he even intended to attack the holy cities of the Hijaz. Yet within a few months of his death, an alternative perspective emerged when the French cleric Peter of Blois (d. 1211) praised Reynald as an exemplary Christian and martyr in the *Passio Reginaldi*, an impassioned piece of crusading propaganda.[2]

It is fair to say that, in crusade historiography as well as in the modern popular imagination, Ibn Shaddad's view has won the day over Peter's: Reynald has become the quintessential bad crusader. With few exceptions, historians since the nineteenth century have portrayed him as at best a reckless brigand, and at worst as a gratuitously cruel barbarian. In 2018, for example, a user of the question-and-answer website *Quora* posted the question 'Why is Reynald de Chatillon so universally disliked in the history of the crusades?'[3] In the English-speaking world, this view was likely cemented by Ridley Scott's 2005 blockbuster *Kingdom of Heaven*, which presents Reynald as at once a greedy brute and a religious fanatic.[4] A few scholars (and non-scholars) have sought to add nuance to his portrayal, and occasionally even to rehabilitate his reputation, but the medieval sources do not leave particularly strong material for his defenders to marshal.[5] In what follows, I will leave aside the debate over whether he deserves his current bad press, and instead focus on how opinions of his career have followed shifting conceptions of the crusades, from Peter of Blois's apocalyptic vision to Ridley Scott's anti-imperialist and anti-fundamentalist framework. It would be impossible to provide a comprehensive 'reception study' in a short chapter, so the following account will simply identify a few representative examples from historiography and popular culture. What should become clear is that, for nearly a millennium, historians and other commentators have found in Reynald's career a useful touchstone for discussing the very meaning of the crusades and the violence they inspired.

Reynald's career as a villain

Reynald's career can be reconstructed from contemporary chronicles in at least six languages, and most historians of the crusades and the Latin East are familiar with the key events of his life.[6] Born around 1125 to a powerful noble family (he was the grandson of Count Geoffrey II of Chalon), he was lord of Châtillon-sur-Loire before traveling to the East with King Louis VII during the Second Crusade.[7] In 1153 he became prince of Antioch when, to the shock of the local nobility, as a relative unknown he married the widow Constance of Antioch. He quarrelled with fellow Franks, the Byzantines, and local church leadership. After a dispute over ecclesiastical funds, he forced the patriarch of Antioch to sit in the baking sun, head uncovered and smeared with honey so that flies might torment him.[8] He then fought on behalf of Emperor Manuel Comnenus, and when Manuel did not pay him for services rendered, he pillaged the Byzantine possession of Cyprus, a crime for which he later had to grovel in submission.[9] He returned to being a general nuisance to many in the region, but when he engaged in what Bernard Hamilton termed 'cattle rustling' west of Edessa in 1161, the Turkish leader Nur ad-Din captured him and put him in prison until 1176, during which time his wife died and his stepson took over the principality.[10]

Upon his release, Reynald secured another fortuitous marriage with an heiress, and this time it snared him the rich lordships of Transjordan and Hebron.[11] Now in command of a great fief in the southeast of the Latin Kingdom of Jerusalem, Reynald was in a position to harass travellers on the caravan routes between Egypt, Damascus, and the Hijaz. He seems to have done so frequently while becoming a prominent adviser, even 'executive regent', to King Baldwin IV.[12] At one point he sent an expedition down the Red Sea, which some Muslim writers saw as part of a campaign against Mecca and Medina.[13] His raids, which sometimes involved breaking truces with the Muslims, garnered him the implacable enmity of Saladin, who promised to kill him with his own hand. After the destruction of the kingdom's army at Hattin, which many historians have blamed on Reynald's reckless truce-breaking, Saladin made good on his promise. According to Ibn Shaddad, the sultan offered Reynald the chance to convert to Islam, and when he refused, 'drew his scimitar and struck him, severing his arm at his shoulder'. In Ibn Shaddad's account, Saladin's guards dragged him out the tent and finished him off, although other chroniclers (both Muslim and Christian) insisted that Saladin killed Reynald with his own hand. [14]

From this brief summary of his life, we can glean a few key examples of the villainy upon which Reynald's poor reputation rests. In the Christian sources for his early career, his three most spectacular offenses – the persecution of the patriarch of Antioch, the plunder of Cyprus, the breaking of truces – seem to be the sort of thing one might expect from a hot-headed Frankish knight. That is, Reynald sometimes resembled the knights we find in anecdotes about violence in the decentralised France of the eleventh and twelfth centuries.[15]

Reynald's contemporary, the great historian William of Tyre, disliked him in part because he was just such an agent of disorder, but also because they represented rival factions in the Latin Kingdom.[16] It is in William's chronicle that we find the germ of the villainous Reynald who became ubiquitous in nineteenth- and twentieth-century crusades historiography. To William, Reynald was essentially a mercenary, a 'knight in the pay of the king' whose treatment of the patriarch showed how easily he could be 'moved to violent and inexcusable wrath'.[17] While admitting that Reynald brought great energy to his endeavours, William feared that his brigandage seriously damaged the Latin cause. Even the relatively sympathetic *Itinerarium Regis Ricardi* places blame for Saladin's 1187 invasion of the Holy Land squarely on Reynald's shoulders, since his attack on a merchant caravan en route from Damascus to Egypt gave the Sultan 'some pretext for declaring war'.[18]

In the eyes of the Arabic chroniclers, however, Reynald was not just violent and reckless but uniquely threatening to Islam. Ibn al Athir (d. 1233) called him 'one of the most devilish and recalcitrant Franks, and the most hostile to Muslims'.[19] This has something to do with their concern to present Reynald's nemesis, Saladin, as the guardian of Islam, but also reflects the growing insistence of many Arabic authors that resistance to the Franks was truly *jihad* on behalf of the faith.[20] Within this framework, Reynald's wickedness is cast in religious terms, nowhere so clearly as in a fourth great example from the list of his nefarious acts, his raid down the Red Sea.

According to mostly Arabic sources, Reynald transported the pieces of five galleys on camels across the Negev desert on camels, then had them assembled and launched on the Gulf of Aqaba in late 1182 or early 1183 (he himself stayed on shore). Eventually they landed near Jedda, close by the holiest sites of Islam. Travel writer Ibn Jubayr (d. 1217), who was passing through the area, thought that they intended to besiege Medina and destroy the tomb of the Prophet; indeed, he argues that they advertised their intent 'and let report of it run on their tongues'.[21] Eventually the ships were hunted down by the admiral Husan al-Din Lu'lu, and the men were captured and executed, some of them publicly outside Mecca.

While it would be easy to dismiss the raid as a bizarre, piratical venture, Hamilton has seen it as part of Reynald's strategic vision for putting pressure on Saladin and his allies.[22] What is clear is that Muslims saw the raid as a threat to the holy sites of the Hijaz, and their language is telling. In a letter to Baghdad recounting the raid and its aftermath, Saladin's advisor al-Fādil (d. 1200) wrote that the Franks 'violated the Red Sea as if it were a virgin' and presented a 'danger to [God's] sacred house [the Ka'bah], the station of Abraham, the legacy of the ancient prophets, and the tomb of His greatest Prophet'.[23] By appealing to the language of sexual pollution as well as sacred geography, al-Fādil turned Saladin and his commanders into defenders of the faith, that is, of a unified Islamic world. Although this letter does not specifically name Reynald as the instigator of the Red Sea raid, Ibn al-Athir had no doubt of who was responsible; he presented the raid as one of the actions that made Reynald Saladin's worst antagonist. Arabic writers, that is, used Reynald the villain to help construct the sultan as a true Islamic hero.[24]

The elephant of Christ? Reynald as martyr and hero

In the Latin West, Reynald's death at Hattin was understood in light of the nearly simultaneous capture of the relic of the True Cross and the subsequent fall of Jerusalem on 2 October 1187. When Pope Gregory VIII completed the bull *Audita tremendi* that called the Third Crusade, he introduced a formula that framed the Hattin catastrophe in terms of the Cross, the city, and the knights who were killed: 'our side was defeated and the Lord's Cross was captured. The bishops were slaughtered, the king captured, and almost all our men were either put to the sword or taken prisoner'.[25] Several chroniclers and preachers of the Third Crusade adopted this formula of linking the loss of knightly lives to the loss of the True Cross. The eyewitness who wrote the *Libellus de expugantione sanctae terrae* specifically named Reynald, along with the Templars and Hospitallers, as Saladin's victims at the time of the Cross's capture, and his death is noted in several other chronicles.[26] Ralph Niger (d. *c*. 1200) wrote that 'the blessed Reynald was killed, protesting that he would not give up a single foot of the Holy Land, even to save his own life'.[27] There is some evidence that a circle of Latin clergy were regarding Reynald as a hero and martyr early on (and Guy of Lusignan would have benefitted from his association with such a martyr), but the clearest extant rendering of Reynald as a pious warrior pilgrim is found in Peter of Blois' *Passio Reginaldi*.[28]

As Christopher Tyerman has argued, it was during the late twelfth century that the crusading ideal began to crystallise around notions of penance, military pilgrimage, and papal leadership.[29] Peter of Blois, in his emotionally powerful *Passio*, integrated Reynald into this model, combining elements of hagiography and apocalyptic preaching into what Alexander Marx has sensibly described as a 'sermon' on penance and the Holy Land rather than a true saint's life.[30] Indeed, given that Peter did not mention Reynald by name until more than 250 lines into the work, it is clear that Peter's real focus was on the fate of the Holy Land and the acts of penance required to recover it. According to Peter, Reynald was, and always had been, an ideal warrior-pilgrim. When he acquired the principality of Antioch through marriage, he vowed to 'fight for the law of God even to his death, for he saw that on this pilgrimage he did not have a city, but ought to seek the one to come' (paraphrasing Hebrews 13:14).[31] Peter also vividly describes the sacred landscape where Reynald lived and fought, placing him at the centre of the Christian world. He was captured 'like another Ezechiel,' and his release is likened to a biblical return from exile.

Like the Arab writers, Peter used Saladin and Reynald as foils for each other. Saladin appears in the *Passsio* as a bumbling tyrant, much like the Roman officials in early Christian martyr narratives. He kills Reynald after being bested in argument, unwittingly granting him the privilege of dying in the presence of the True Cross. According to Peter, they debated in Arabic (not implausible given Reynald's lengthy stay in Nur ad-Din's prison) before a frustrated Saladin declared 'my own hand will kill this man who dared to blaspheme against my glorious majesty'.[32] Refusing to save his life by converting to Islam, Reynald accepted death gallantly, contemplating the Cross (this is in stark contrast to the death scene in Ibn Shaddad's life of Saladin, in which a dehydrated Reynald attempts to partake of a cup of ice proffered to King Guy).[33] Jay Rubenstein has recently noted that Peter's *Passio*, by turning a military foe of Islam into a martyr, represented a major innovation, one that was 'almost unprecedented' in crusading literature.[34] Peter skilfully deployed the biblical allusions common to crusading propaganda, as well as its language of penitential pilgrimage, to create an emotionally appealing hero.[35]

Reynald and the historians

Reynald of Châtillon did not figure prominently in later medieval crusades chronicles, but he appears in most of the standard histories of the crusades written since the sixteenth century. Johannes Herold's *De bello sacro* (1560), following William of Tyre closely, describes Reynald as a trucebreaker and a 'man of great spirit, greedy for spoils,' in just the sort of portrayal that would reverberate throughout the next five centuries.[36] Herold read the crusades through the lens of contemporary conflicts between Christians and Ottoman Turks, and perhaps as a result treated Reynald's fate as a cautionary tale.[37] At nearly the same time, John Foxe included a somewhat muddled account of Reynald (whom he names 'Raymond the Prince'), in his *Book of Martyrs*. Here, the prince of Antioch represents the 'dissension among the Christian states of Palestine', which allowed Saladin to conquer Jerusalem.[38]

Nineteenth- and twentieth-century historians continued to portray Reynald as a man of great energy with a cruel streak. In Joseph François Michaud's famously 'romantic' *Histoire des croisades* (1811–22), we learn that Reynald's first wife Constance had been captivated by his 'beauty and chivalric bravery', but also that '[h]eedless of the rights of nations or humanity, he imprisoned women and children, and massacred unarmed men'.[39] Consistent with his view of crusading as an arena in which Christian men could act virtuously, Michaud measured Reynald based on his alternating conformity to, and deviation from, a newly invented chivalric ethos. Many other histories of the nineteenth century clearly followed the template set by William of Tyre, but the concerns of contemporary historiography crept into representations of the prince of Antioch. At the start of the twentieth century W.B. Stevenson, well versed in Arabic sources and often critical of the Franks, portrayed Reynald as a high-spirited truce breaker, but also cast a somewhat sceptical eye on earlier historians who had 'too exclusively' cast the blame for Hattin on Reynald.[40] The French historian Gustave Schlumberger wrote a rare flattering account of Reynald's career in 1898, which stood more clearly in the tradition of the nineteenth-century Romantics than those writing crusade histories at the turn of the century.[41] Though it received a positive review in the *Bibliothèque de l'École des Chartes* when it appeared, it did little to rehabilitate Reynald's reputation in the eyes of mainstream scholars.[42]

The tensions that would inform later debates over Reynald are most spectacularly demonstrated in works associated with what Tyerman has called the 'Franco-German colonial model'. For the historians who constructed this model, the crusades prefigured nineteenth-century imperialism; in Tyerman's words, these scholars saw the Frankish settlements as an opportunity for 'mutually beneficial colonial harmony'.[43] Perhaps reflecting on colonial unrest in Algeria, the Frenchman René Grousset, writing in 1935, saw in Reynald an embodiment of the worst kind of colonial, an opportunist who barged in and destroyed the good work of the settlers who had been there longer. Reynald presented a 'mortal danger' (*péril mortel*) to the Franks who had established themselves after 1099 and assimilated to their environs.[44] In this reading, Reynald was less a villain than an example of how to perform settler colonialism badly. Like William of Tyre, Grousset regretted that Reynald unwittingly worked against Frankish interests, but what was truly tragic was that he undermined what could have been benevolent Frankish (or, perhaps, French) rule.

In the post-war period, as academic crusading historiography took off in radically new directions, Steven Runciman featured Reynald prominently in his three-volume *A History of the Crusades* (1951–4). He followed Grousset in comparing Reynald unfavourably with the Franks who had already settled in the Holy Land: he was one of the 'newcomers from the West, aggressive, unadapted'.[45] While Grousset thought Reynald's cultural insensitivity and brutishness spoiled the chance for an enlightened imperial project, Runciman found in him the perfect exemplar of the crusading movement's 'sin against the Holy Ghost'.[46] Reynald 'shocked his fellow believers' with his brutality, inflicted a wound on Cyprus from which the then-Byzantine possession 'never recovered'.[47] When Reynald allegedly turned his sights on Mecca and Medina, 'the whole Moslem world was horrified'.[48] All of this fitted perfectly with Runciman's central thesis that the crusades were a tragic blunder that betrayed Christian ideals, alienated the Muslim world, and crippled the Greek East that he so admired. Again, Reynald of Châtillon epitomised everything that was fundamentally wrong with crusading.

According to most accounts of crusading historiography, the key development since Runciman's *History* has been the re-affirmation of religious ideas as central to crusading. This 'neo-religious explanation', as Kristin Skottki has called it, has taken seriously the religious ideas of crusaders and minimised their political or material interests in traveling to the Holy Land.[49] Although Peter of Blois's *Passio Reginaldi* powerfully demonstrates trends in crusading spirituality, it is somewhat difficult to fit Reynald himself into any account of twelfth-century piety. As a result, for the past few decades historians have described Reynald in language that recalls his original medieval critics. He has been deemed an 'adventurer' and an opportunist, and a 'fanatical crusader buccaneer', among other things.[50] Historian Brian Catlos, who is less comfortable than many medievalists with the neo-religious explanation, de-emphasised the crusaders' religious motivations in *Infidel Kings and Unholy Warriors*. Seeing religion as a mask for more worldly pursuits, argues that Reynald in particular 'epitomized the self-serving ambitions of late-coming Latins'.[51]

The few scholars that have looked for redeeming qualities in Reynald have tended to argue that, as a strategist and warrior, Reynald was actually fairly good at what he did. Ronnie Ellenblum, for example, contrasted his

Reynald of Châtillon 49

'heroic attempt [...] to raid the Hijaz' with the cautious inaction of other commanders for the Latin Kingdom.[52] Hamilton and others have argued that Reynald's seemingly reckless raids were part of a plan to embarrass Saladin and force him to divert resources from northern Syria.[53] While there has been little inclination among historians for a thorough 'rehabilitation' of Reynald, Hamilton and Carole Hillenbrand have sought to understand his motivations and to consider him as a committed defender of Christian interests, that is, as an enthusiastic crusader. Scrutinising Reynald's actions against Saladin in the 1170s and '80s, Hamilton suggested that after his imprisonment Reynald for the first time became 'sincerely committed to the crusader cause'.[54] In his mildly revisionist 1978 article Hamilton termed Reynald 'the Elephant of Christ', referring back to the Qur'an's story of an Ethiopian Christian king who attacked Mecca with elephants in 570 (Sura 105). Some Muslims saw this earlier invader as a prefiguration of the lord of Kerak, suggesting that they took Reynald's crusading zeal seriously. Taking a slightly different tack on the problem of Reynald's motivation, Hillenbrand argued, somewhat speculatively, that Reynald could have emerged from the psychological trauma of his captivity bent on revenge.[55] If Hillenbrand is correct that Reynald saw his attacks on Muslims as an act of repentance for earlier sins, then one could reasonably fit him into the mainstream of contemporary crusading ideology.

Reynald, film, and the clash of civilizations

During the same decades when most crusade historians left behind the older colonial paradigms, brokers of popular culture such as journalists, video game designers, filmmakers, and others have often diverged from scholarly consensus. Their work often reflects the continuing influence of Runciman's work, or reaches back even further to the nineteenth-century novelists who regaled readers with stories of barbarous Franks and sophisticated, civilised Muslims. Reynald has received consistent attention, often as a proxy for contemporary political concerns. Chief among these are the Palestinian-Israeli conflict, the United States' military incursions into the Islamic world, and the legacy of European imperialism in the Middle East. Some have made very direct comparisons between Reynald and modern actors. According to a conversation related by the late peace activist Uri Avnery, Runciman himself identified Reynald as the precursor of Israeli defence minister Moshe Dayan, while Karen Armstrong likened him to the Jewish terrorists who plotted to blow up the Dome of the Rock and the al-Aqsa mosque in 1984.[56]

In the Arab world, few have presented Reynald as an imperialist villain more effectively than Egyptian Christian filmmaker Youssef Chahine did in his 1963 epic *El Naser Salah Ad-Din* ('Saladin the Victorious').[57] Filming at the height of the era of the Egyptian President Gamal Nasser, and less than a decade after the Suez Crisis of 1956, Chahine viewed the crusades as attempts to expropriate Arab resources, and the crusaders as boorish ingrates attacking a superior civilization.[58] In one scene at the court of the king of France, a princess practically bathes in jewellery while exhorting the king to undertake a crusade to recover the 'treasures of the East'. Others, 'enchanted by the magic of the East,' seem to be models of naïve orientalism. Saladin promises to protect all the residents of Jerusalem, which according to an Arabic Christian character, 'has always been on Arab land'. Reynald himself, depicted as the chief commander of the Christian armies, is relatively young, impetuous, and utterly devoid of the chivalry displayed by the hero Saladin. In an extraordinary scene which merges his attack on a merchant caravan with the Red Sea raid, he and his knights slaughter white-clad pilgrims precisely because they are unarmed, so he can easily take their goods to replenish his empty treasury at Kerak. When captured, Saladin does not execute him but kills him after an extended duel sequence nearly worthy of Scaramouche. Ironically, Reynald does not conform to western ideals of chivalry as well as Saladin does. For Chahine, Reynald represented a dangerous European threat that could only be countered by the kind of 'Arab' unity effected in the twelfth century by the Kurdish Saladin and in the twentieth by Nasser. On a more positive note, Saladin looks forward to an Arab modernity unimpeded by Western imperialism.[59]

Saladin and Reynald continued to be linked in the popular imagination in the decades after Chahine's film, perhaps most poignantly in front of the Citadel in Damascus. There, in 1993, Syrian president Hafez Assad dedicated a monumental group sculpture of the Kurdish commander on horseback.[60] Reynald's defeat thwarted an attack not just on Arab territory but on Islam itself, and so the piece reflects a take on what is often called a 'clash of civilizations' between Islam and the West.[61]

One notable exponent of the 'clash' thesis, Bernard Lewis, invoked Reynald's memory in a 1998 article in *Foreign Affairs*. Nearly three years before the attacks of 11 September 2001, Lewis argued that the past actions of 'infidels' like Reynald provided essential background for understanding the forces that motivated the terrorism of Osama bin Laden and those like him.[62] In the aftermath of those attacks and the subsequent US invasion of Iraq, particularly once President George W. Bush had labelled the 'War on Terror' a 'crusade', journalists and scholars considered the role of religious fundamentalism in fomenting military conflict with renewed urgency.

It was in this context that Reynald reached a new Anglophone audience in 2005, when the English director Ridley Scott released *Kingdom of Heaven*, an epic about the events leading up to the Third Crusade.[63] Scott's

Reynald (played by Brendan Gleeson) is a reckless aggressor responsible for the loss of Jerusalem, and a religious fundamentalist in league with the Templars (he is even referred to as 'Templar bastard'); he is both an imperialist and a bigot. One of Scott's more interesting choices was to contrast Reynald's bigotry not only with Saladin's religious tolerance but also with the more enlightened colonialism of Tiberias (clearly representing the historical Raymond of Tripoli) and King Baldwin IV, who in the film strive to treat the local Muslims fairly. Tiberias and Baldwin try desperately to bring Reynald to heel, but to no avail: Saladin takes his revenge by executing Reynald, and Jerusalem is lost.

Reynald thus embodies all the forces in the twelfth-century Levant, and the twenty-first-century United States, that have stood in the way of interreligious harmony. Some academic historians objected not only to Scott's distortions of the historical record, but also to his approach to medieval religion in general. Thomas Madden, in a review for the conservative *National Review* titled 'Onward PC Soldiers', summarised the moral of the film as 'Religion leads to fanaticism, and fanaticism leads to war.'[64] The doyen of Anglophone crusade historians, Jonathan Riley-Smith, lamented in an interview with the *Telegraph* that the film represented 'Osama bin Laden's version of history', presumably by positioning the crusaders like Reynald as precursors to modern, anti-Muslim imperialists.[65] While these historians objected to Scott's somewhat rosy view of medieval religious tolerance, it is certainly possible to reject *Kingdom of Heaven's* project as itself orientalising. After all, not only did Scott's idealised characterisations of Saladin and Baldwin conform to highly secularised Western notions of an enlightened leader, but he also helped construct a twelfth-century Holy Land where the fictional Tiberias's vision of settler colonialism seems benign. As Richard Schlimm has argued, '*Kingdom of Heaven* characterizes Islam in terms of post-Christian spirituality, undermining some of the most fundamental tenets of Islam.'[66] Reynald becomes the 'bad apple' that allows Western viewers to justify European and US imperial projects.

Conclusion

Ridley Scott's film was hardly the last word on Reynald of Châtillon in the twenty-first century, as he continues to appear in popular culture in his traditional role as trucebreaker who doomed the Latin Kingdom of Jerusalem, but occasionally as an unfairly pilloried hero who needs to be rescued from disrepute. The digital age has embraced him in video games like *Crusader Kings* and in internet chat rooms discussing history and politics. In the discussion boards of the 'Middle East Forum', the website of historian-turned pundit Daniel Pipes, a user with the handle 'Reynald de Chatillon' has urged

52 *John D. Cotts*

Israel to annex the former territories of 'the united monarchy of David and Solomon' and to expel the Muslim population.⁶⁷

Just four years ago, Reynald received what is essentially a modern hagiography in journalist Jeffrey Lee's *God's Wolf*. In his conclusion, Lee assures readers that 'above all, [Reynald] was loyal, he was brave, he was a soldier, well versed in war'.⁶⁸ Lee found some sympathetic readers like the political blogger James Delingpole, who praised Reynald as 'the greatest crusader' and blamed Reynald's bad press on 'cultural self-hatred mixed with a sort of embarrassed, well-meaning politeness designed to make Muslims feel less chippy about their historical heritage'. Lee's attempt at rehabilitation has, however, been ignored or (rightly) panned by historians. Reviewing *God's Wolf*, Matthew Gabriele criticised Lee for implying that the crusades lived on today, and characterising the book in general as 'just awful.'⁶⁹ Islamist terrorists too have found in Reynald a potent symbol of what they fight against, most notably in 2010 when two mail bombs were discovered in cargo planes bound from Yemen, one of them addressed to 'Reynald Krak'.⁷⁰

Clearly, Reynald of Châtillon's career still resonates today, perhaps because he so energetically carved out a place for himself in the politics of the region which is still the subject of most discussions of religious violence. To label him a villain is to commit no anachronism, for he has been so labelled since relatively early in his own lifetime. Moreover, the same acts that have made him so reviled should resonate in contemporary discussions of settler colonialism. Those who have found him a hero include those who embraced the crusading project as Peter of Blois did, but also those today like Lee who focus on military and 'chivalrous' components of the crusades. What I hope this survey has demonstrated is that the paradigms historians choose for considering crusading violence (e.g. imperialism, piety, romanticism) truly matter. Ideally, we can use those paradigms to create new possibilities for confronting contemporary violence.

Notes

1 Bahā' al-Dīn Ibn Shaddad, *The Rare and Excellent History of Saladin*, trans. D.S. Richards (Aldershot, 2001), pp. 37, 74–5.
2 Peter of Blois, *Passio Reginaldi*, in *Petrus Blesensis Tractatus Duo*, ed. R.B.C. Huygens (Turnhout, 2002).
3 Anonymous, 'Why is Reynald de Chatillon so Universally disliked in the history of the Crusades?', *Quora*, <https://www.quora.com/Why-is-Reynald-de-Chatillon-so-universally-disliked-in-the-history-of-the-Crusades>, [accessed 21 August 2019].
4 *Kingdom of Heaven*, DVD, directed by Ridley Scott (Hollywood, 2012).
5 The most prominent example is Jeffrey Lee, *God's Wolf* (New York, 2016), p. 298. See also James Delingpole, 'Who Remembers the Greatest Crusader?', *The*

Spectator, 28 July 2018, <https://www.spectator.co.uk/2018/07/who-remembers-the-greatest-crusader/amp/>, [accessed 20 February 2020].
6 In addition to the Latin and Arabic sources cited in this article see also Bar Hebraeus, *Chronography*, trans. Ernest A. Wallis Budge (Oxford, 1932), p. 324; John Kinnamos, *The Deeds of John and Manuel Comnenus*, trans. C.M. Brand (New York, 1976), pp. 137–40, 142, 151, 164; Matthew of Edessa, *Armenia and the Crusades*, trans. Ara E. Doustorian (London, 1993), p. 272.
7 This summary draws primarily on Bernard Hamilton, 'The Elephant of Christ: Reynald of Châtillon' in *Religious Motivation* (Oxford, 1978), pp. 97–108; and Hamilton, *The Leper King and His Heirs* (Cambridge, 2000), pp. 104–5.
8 William of Tyre, *Chronicon*, ed. R.B.C. Huygens, vol. 2 (Turnhout, 1986), p. 809.
9 Hamilton, *Leper King*, p. 104.
10 Hamilton, 'Elephant', p. 98.
11 Carole Hillenbrand, 'Some Reflections on the Imprisonment of Reynald of Châtillon' in *Texts, Documents, and Artefacts*, eds. C.F. Robinson and Chase F. Robinson (Leiden, 2003), pp. 79–102.
12 Hamilton, *Leper King*, p. 118.
13 Ibid, pp. 179–84; Marcus Milwright, 'Reynald of Châtillon and the Red Sea Raid of 1182–83' in *Noble Ideals and Bloody Realities*, eds. Niall Christie and Maya Yazigi (Leiden, 2005), pp. 235–60; Alex Mallett, 'A Trip Down the Red Sea with Reynald of Châtillon', *Journal of the Royal Asiatic Society*, 3rd ser., 18 (2008), pp. 141–53; William Facey, 'Crusaders in the Red Sea: Renaud de Châtillon's Raids of AD 1182–1183', in *People of the Red Sea*, ed. Janet C.M. Starkey (Oxford, 2005), pp. 87–98.
14 Ibn Shaddad, *Saladin*, p. 75. On the accounts of his death, see Hamilton, 'Elephant', p. 107.
15 See, for example, Thomas N. Bisson, *The Crisis of the Twelfth Century* (Princeton, NJ, 2009), esp. pp. 62–68.
16 See Philp D. Handyside, 'Differing Views of Renaud de Châtillon: William of Tyre and *L'Estoire d'Eracles*', in *Deeds Done Beyond the Sea* (Aldershot, 2014), pp. 43–52; Hamilton, 'Elephant', p. 97.
17 William of Tyre, *Chronicon*, p. 809; translated as *History of Deeds Done Beyond the Sea*, trans. August C. Krey (New York, 1943), 2, p. 235.
18 *Itinerarium peregrinorum et Gesta Regis Ricardi*, in *Chronicles and Memorials of the Reign of Richard I*, ed. William Stubbs, Rolls Series 38.2 (London, 1865), p. 11, translated as *The Chronicle of the Third Crusade: The Itinerarium Peregrinorum et Gesta Regis Ricardi*, ed. Helen J. Nicholson (Aldershot, 1997), p. 29.
19 *The Chronicle of Ibn al-Athīr for the Crusading Period from al-Kāmil fīta'rīkh, Part 2*, trans. D.S. Richards (Aldershot, 2007), p. 276.
20 See Carole Hillenbrand, *The Crusades* (London, 1999), pp. 171–87.
21 Ibn Jubayr, *The Travels of Ibn Jubayr*, trans. R.J.C. Broadhurst (London, 1952), p. 52.
22 Hamilton, *Leper King*, pp. 181–4.
23 Quoted in Gary La Viere Leiser, 'The Crusader Raid in the Red Sea in 578/1182-83', *Journal of the American Research Center in Egypt* 14 (1977), p. 91.
24 See especially Hannes Möhring, *Saladin*, trans. David Bachrach (Baltimore, 2008), p. 60; and Anne-Marie Eddé, *Saladin*, trans. Jane Marie Todd (Cambridge, MA, 2011), pp. 370–1.

25 *Audita tremendi*, in *Patrologia Latina*, ed. J.-P. Migne, vol. 202 (Paris, 1855), col. 1540.
26 *Libellus de expugnatione sanctae terrae*, in *Radulphi de Coggeshall Chronicon Anglicanum*, ed. Joseph Stevenson (London, 1875), p. 228.
27 *Radulfus Niger – Chronica: Eine englische Weltchronik des 12. Jahrhunderts*, ed. Hanna Krause (Frankfurt am Main, 1986), pp. 278–9.
28 See Christopher Tyerman, *God's War* (Cambridge, MA, 2006), p. 407; Bernard Hamilton, 'The Old French Translation of William of Tyre' in *The Experience of Crusading, Volume Two*, eds. Peter Edbury and Jonathan Phillips (Cambridge, 2003), p. 111.
29 Christopher Tyerman, 'Were There Any Crusades in the Twelfth Century?' in *The Invention of the Crusades* (Toronto, 1998), pp. 8–29.
30 Alexander Marx, 'Die Passio Raginaldi von Petrus von Blois: Märtyrertum, Emotionalität und Eschatologie', MA thesis (University of Vienna, 2014), pp. 14–19.
31 'Videbat enim quod non habebat in hac perigrinatione manentem civitatem, sed futuram oportebat inquiri', Peter of Blois, *Passio Reginaldi*, p. 43.
32 'qui mee gloriam maiestatis ausus est blasphemare, interficiet manus mea', ibid., p. 59.
33 Ibn Shaddad, *Saladin*, p. 75.
34 Rubenstein, *Nebuchadnezzar's Dream* (Oxford, 2019), p. 173.
35 See, in addition to Rubenstein, above, John D. Cotts 'The Exegesis of Violence in the Crusade Writings of Ralph Niger and Peter of Blois' in *The Uses of the Bible in Crusader Sources*, eds. Elizabeth Lapina and Nicholas Morton (Leieden, 2017), pp. 273–95.
36 Johannes Herold, *De bello sacro* (Basel, 1560), p. 9.
37 See Christopher Tyerman, *The Debate on the Crusades* (Manchester, 2011), pp. 39–40.
38 *Foxe's Book of Martyrs*, ed. John Cumming, vol. I (London, 1851), p. 1125. Again, see Tyerman, *Debate*, pp. 40–2.
39 Joseph François Michaud, *The History of the Crusades*, vol. 3, trans. W. Robson, (New York, 1882), pp. 403, 405.
40 W.B. Stevenson, *The Crusaders in the East* (Cambridge, 1907), pp. 240–1.
41 Gustave Schlumberger, *Renaud de Châtillon, Prince d'Antioche, Seigneur de la Terre d'Outre-Jourdain*, 2nd ed. (Paris, 1923).
42 M. Prou, review of Shlumberger's *Renaud de Châtillon*, in *Bibliothèque de l'École des Chartes* 59 (1898), pp. 603–7.
43 Tyerman, *Debate*, p. 116.
44 René Grousset, *Histoire des Croisades et du Royaume Franc de Jérusalem. Tome 2* (Paris, 1935), pp. 331–2.
45 Runciman, *Crusades*, 2, p. 186.
46 Ibid., 3, p. 480.
47 Ibid., 2, pp. 319, 348.
48 Ibid., 2, p. 437.
49 Kristin Skottki, 'The Dead, the Revived and the Recreated Pasts: "Structural Amnesia" in Representations of Crusade History' in *Engaging the Crusades, Vol. 1*, p. 113.
50 Tyerman, *God's War*, pp. 195–6; Hillenbrand, *The Crusades*, p. 296.
51 Brian Catlos, *Infidel Kings and Unholy Warriors* (New York, 2014), p. 277.
52 Ronnie Ellenblum, *Crusader Castles and Modern Histories* (Cambridge, 2007), p. 278.

53 Hamilton, 'Elephant', p. 102.
54 Ibid., p. 99.
55 Hillenbrand, 'Reflections', pp. 98–101.
56 Uri Avnery,'Parallels Between Crusaders and Zionists', *Arab News,* 11 October 2014, <www.arabnews.com/columns/news/642231>; Karen Armstrong, *Holy War* (New York, 1991), p. 273.
57 *El Naser Salah Ad-Din*, directed by Youssef Chahine (Egypt, 1963).
58 For short but comprehensive introductions to the film, see Paul B. Sturtevant, 'SaladiNasser: Nasser's Political Crusade in *El Naser Salah Ad-Din*' in *Hollywood in the Holy Land*, pp. 123–46; John Aberth, *A Knight at the Movies* (New York, 2003), pp. 91–107.
59 John M. Ganim, 'Reversing the Crusades: Hegemony, Orientalism, and Film Language in Youssef Chahine's *Saladin*' in *Race, Class, and Gender in Medieval Cinema*, eds. Lynn T. Ramey and Tison Pugh (Basingstoke, 2007), p. 51.
60 See Hillenbrand, *The Crusades*, pp. 595–600; Anthony Pagden, *Worlds at War* (New York, 2008), p. 241.
61 See the comprehensive formulation in Samuel P. Huntingdon, *The Clash of Civilizations and the Remaking of World Order* (New York, 1996), and a volume of essays debating the subject in Huntingdon, ed., *The Clash of Civilizations? The Debate* (New York, 1996).
62 Bernard Lewis, 'Usama Bin Ladin's Declaration of Jihad', *Foreign Affairs* 77:6 (November/December 1998), pp. 14–19.
63 On the film, see Lorraine Kochanske Stock, 'Now Starring in the Third Crusade' in *Hollywood in the Holy Land*, pp. 97–122. For another view of the film and the response to it, see Paul Sturtevant, 'Kingdom of Heaven's Road Map for Peace', *Bulletin of International Medieval Research* 12 (2006), pp. 23–40.
64 Thomas F. Madden, 'Onward PC Soldiers', *The National Review*, 27 May 2005, <https://www.nationalreview.com/2005/05/onward-pc-soldiers-thomas-f-madden/>, [accessed 20 May 2019].
65 Charlotte Edwards, 'Ridley Scott's new Crusades film 'panders to Osama bin Laden', *The Telegraph*, 18 January 2004, <www.telegraph.co.uk/news/world news/northamerica/usa/1452000/Ridley-Scotts-new-Crusades-film-panders-to-Osama-bin-Laden.html>, [accessed 20 May 2019].
66 Matthew Richard Schlimm, 'The Necessity of Permanent Criticism: A Postcolonial Critique of Ridley Scott's *Kingdom of Heaven*', *Journal of Media and Religion* 9 (2010), p. 145.
67 Anonymous, 'Illusion of Peace', *Middle East Forum*, <http://www.danielpipes.org/comments/242598>, [accessed 6 September 2019].
68 Lee, *God's Wolf*, p. 298.
69 Matthew Gabriele, 'Review of *God's Wolf*, by Jeffrey Lee', *The Historian* 80 (2018), pp. 612–13.
70 Mark Mazetti and Scott Shane, 'In Parcel Bomb Plot, 2 Dark Inside Jokes', *New York Times*, 2 November 2010, <https://www.nytimes.com/2010/11/03/world/03terror.html>, [accessed 10 June 2019].

Bibliography

Primary

Anonymous. *Itinerarium peregrinorum* et *Gesta Regis Ricardi*. In *Chronicles and Memorials of the Reign of Richard I*. ed. William Stubbs. Rolls Series 38.2.

London: Longman, 1865. Trans. as *The Chronicle of the Third Crusade: The Itinerarium Peregrinorum et Gesta Regis Ricardi*. ed. Helen J. Nicholson, Crusade Texts in Translation 3. Aldershot: Ashgate, 1997.

Anonymous. *Libellus de expugnatione sanctae terrae*. In *Radulphi de Coggeshall Chronicon Anglicanum*. ed. Joseph Stevenson. Rolls Series 66. London: Longman, 1875.

Bahā' al-Dīn Ibn Shaddad. *The Rare and Excellent History of Saladin*. Trans. D.S. Richards. Crusade Texts in Translation 7. Aldershot: Ashgate, 2001.

Bar Hebraeus. *Chronography*. Trans. Ernest A. Wallis Budge. Vol. 1. Oxford and London: OUP and Humphrey Milford, 1932.

Gregory VIII. *Audita tremendi*. In *Patrologia Latina*. ed. J.-P. Migne. Vol. 202. Paris, 1855, cols. 1539–42.

Ibn al-Athir. *The Chronicle of Ibn al-Athīr for the Crusading Period from al-Kāmil fīta'rīkh, Part 2*. Trans. D.S. Richards. Crusades Texts in Translation 15. Aldershot: Ashgate, 2007.

Ibn Jubayr. *The Travels of Ibn Jubayr*. Trans. R.J.C. Broadhurst. London: Jonathan Cape, 1952.

John Kinnamos. *The Deeds of John and Manuel Comnenus*. Trans. C.M. Brand. New York: Columbia University Press, 1976.

Matthew of Edessa. *Armenia and the Crusades: The Chronicle of Matthew of Edessa*. Trans. Ara E. Doustorian. Lanham, MD: University Press of America, 1993.

Peter of Blois. *Passio Reginaldi*. In *Petrus Blesensis Tractatus Duo*. ed. R.B.C. Huygens. Corpus Christianorum Continuatio Mediaevalis 194. Turnhout: Brepols, 2002.

Ralph Niger. *Radulfus Niger — Chronica: Eine englische Weltchronik des 12. Jahrhunderts*. Ed. Hanna Krause. Frankfurt am Main: Peter Land, 1986.

William of Tyre. *Chronicon*. Ed. R.B.C. Huygens. Vol. 2. Corpus Christianorum Continuatio Mediaevalis 63a. Turnhout: Brepols, 1986.

Secondary

Aberth, John. *A Knight at the Movies: Medieval History on Film*. New York: McFarland, 2003.

Anonymous. 'Illusion of Peace'. *Middle East Forum*. www.danielpipes.org/comments/242598. [Accessed 6 September 2019].

Anonymous. 'Why is Reynald de Chatillon so Universally disliked in the history of the Crusades?' *Quora*. https://www.quora.com/Why-is-Reynald-de-Chatillon-so-universally-disliked-in-the-history-of-the-Crusades. [Accessed 14 August 2019].

Armstrong, Karen. *Holy War: The Crusades and Their Impact on Today's World*. New York: Anchor Books, 1991.

Avnery, Uri. 'Parallels Between Crusaders and Zionists'. *Arab News*, 11 October 2014. www.arabnews.com/columns/news/642231. [Accessed 6 September 2019].

Bisson, Thomas N. *The Crisis of the Twelfth Century: Power, Lordship, and the Origins of European Government*. Princeton, NJ: Princeton University Press, 2009.

Catlos, Brian. *Infidel Kings and Unholy Warriors: Faith, Power, and Violence in the Age of Crusade and Jihad*. New York: Farrar, Straus and Giroux, 2014.
Cotts, John D. 'The Exegesis of Violence in the Crusade Writings of Ralph Niger and Peter of Blois'. In *The Uses of the Bible in Crusader Sources*. eds. Elizabeth Lapina and Nicholas Morton. Leieden: Brill, 2017, pp. 273–95.
Delingpole, James. 'Who Remembers the Greatest Crusader?' *The Spectator*, 28 July 2018. https://www.spectator.co.uk/2018/07/who-remembers-the-greatest-crusader/amp/. Accessed 20 February 2020.
Eddé, Anne-Marie. *Saladin*, trans. Jane Marie Todd. Cambridge, MA: Harvard University Press, 2011.
Edwards, Charlotte. 'Ridley Scott's new Crusades film 'panders to Osama bin Laden'. *The Telegraph*. 18 January 2004. www.telegraph.co.uk/news/world news/northamerica/usa/1452000/Ridley-Scotts-new-Crusades-film-panders-to-Osama-bin-Laden.html. [Accessed 20 May 2019].
Ellenblum, Ronnie. *Crusader Castles and Modern Histories*. Cambridge: CUP, 2007.
Facey, William. 'Crusaders in the Red Sea: Renaud de Châtillon's Raids of AD 1182–1183'. In *People of the Red Sea: Proceedings of the Red Sea Project II*. ed. Janet C.M. Starkey. Oxford: Archaeopress, 2005, pp. 87–98.
Foxe, John. *Foxe's Book of Martyrs*. Ed. John Cumming. Vol. 1. London, 1851.
Ganim, John M. 'Reversing the Crusades: Hegemony, Orientalism, and Film Language in Youssef Chahine's *Saladin*'. In *Race, Class, and Gender in Medieval Cinema*. eds. Lynn T. Ramey and Tison Pugh. Basingstoke: Palgrave Macmillan, 2007, pp. 45–58.
Grousset, René. *Histoire des Croisades et du Royaume Franc de Jérusalem. Tome 2: Monarchie Franque et Monarchie Musulman L'Équilibre*. Paris: Perrin, 1935.
Hamilton, Bernard. 'The Elephant of Christ: Reynald of Châtillon'. In *Religious Motivation: Biographical and Sociological Problems for the Church Historian*. Studies in Church History 15. ed. Derek Baker. Oxford: Basil Blackwell, 1978, pp. 97–108.
———. *The Leper King and His Heirs: The Reign of Baldwin IV and the Crusader Kingdom of Jerusalem*. Cambridge: CUP, 2000.
———. 'The Old French Translation of William of Tyre'. In *The Experience of Crusading. Volume Two: Defining the Crusader Kingdom*. eds. Peter Edbury and Jonathan Phillips. Cambridge: CUP, 2003.
Handyside, Phillip D. 'Differing Viwes of Renaud de Châtillon: William of Tyre and *L'Estoire d'Eracles*'. In *Deeds Done Beyond the Sea: Essays on William of Tyre, Cyprus and the Military Orders Presented to Peter Edbury*. eds. Susan B. Edgington and Helen J. Nicholson. Aldershot: Ashgate, 2014, pp. 43–52.
Herold, Johannes. *De bello sacro*. Basel: Nicholas Brylingerus, 1560.
Hillenbrand, Carole. *The Crusades: Islamic Perspectives*. London: Fitzroy Dearborn Publishers, 1999.
———. 'Some Reflections on the Imprisonment of Reynald of Châtillon'. In *Texts, Documents, and Artefacts: Islamic Studies in Honour of D.S. Richards*. eds. C.F. Robinson and Chase F. Robinson, Leiden: Brill, 2003, pp. 79–102.

Huntingdon, Samuel P. *The Clash of Civilizations and the Remaking of World Order.* New York: Simon and Schuster, 1996.

———. ed. *The Clash of Civilizations? The Debate.* New York: Foreign Affairs, 1996.

Lee, Jeffrey. *God's Wolf: The Life of the Most Notorious of All Crusaders, Scourge of Saladin.* New York, 2016.

Leiser, Gary La Viere. 'The Crusader Raid in the Red Sea in 578/1182-83'. *Journal of the American Research Center in Egypt* 14 (1977), pp. 87–100.

Lewis, Bernard. 'Usama Bin Ladin's Declaration of Jihad'. *Foreign Affairs* 77.6 (November/December 1998), pp. 14–19.

Madden, Thomas F. 'Onward PC Soldiers'. *The National Review*, 27 May 2005. www.nationalreview.com/2005/05/onward-pc-soldiers-thomas-f-madden. [Accessed 20 May 2019].

Mallett, Alex. 'A Trip Down the Red Sea with Reynald of Châtillon'. *Journal of the Royal Asiatic Society*, 3rd ser., 18 (2008), pp. 141–53.

Marx, Alexander. 'Die Passio Raginaldi von Petrus von Blois: Märtyrertum, Emotionalität und Eschatologie'. MA thesis. University of Vienna, 2014.

Michaud, Joseph François. *The History of the Crusades.* Trans. W. Robson. Vol. 3. New York: A.C. Armstrong and Son, 1882.

Milwright, Marcus. 'Reynald of Châtillon and the Red Sea Raid of 1182–83'. In *Noble Ideals and Bloody Realities: Warfare in the Middle Ages.* eds. Nial Christie and Maya Yazigi. Leiden: Brill, 2005, pp. 235–60.

Möhring, Hans. *Saladin: The Sultan and his Times, 1138–1193.* Trans. David Bachrach. Baltimore, MD: Johns Hopkins University Press, 2008.

Pagden, Anthony. *Worlds at War: The 2,500-Year Struggle Between East and West.* New York: Random House, 2008.

Prou, M. 'Review of Gustave Schlumberger, Renaud de Châtillon, Prince d'Antioche, Seigneur de la Terre d'Outre-Jourdain'. *Bibliothèque de l'Ecole des Chartes* 59 (1898), pp. 603–607.

Rubenstein, Jay. *Nebudchadnezzar's Dream: The Crusades, Apocalyptic Prophecy, and the End of History.* Oxford: OUP, 2019.

Runciman, Steven, *A History of the Crusades.* 3 Vols. Cambridge: CUP, 1951–54.

Schlimm, Matthew Richard. 'The Necessity of Permanent Criticism: A Postcolonial Critique of Ridley Scott's *Kingdom of Heaven*'. *Journal of Media and Religion* 9 (2010), pp. 129–49.

Schlumberger, Gustave. *Renaud de Châtillon, Prince d'Antioche, Seigneur de la Terre d'Outre-Jourdain.* 2nd ed. Paris: Libraire Plon, 1923.

Skottki, Kristin. 'The Dead, the Revived and the Recreated Pasts: 'Structural Amnesia' in Representations of Crusade History'. In *Perceptions of the Crusades from the Nineteenth to the Twenty-First Century: Engaging the Crusades.* Vol. 1. eds. Mike Horswell and Jonathan Phillips. Abingdon: Routledge, 2018, pp. 107–32.

Stevenson, W.B. *The Crusaders in the East.* Cambridge: CUP, 1907.

Stock, Lorraine Kochanske. 'Now Starring in the Third Crusade.' In *Hollywood in the Holy Land: Essays on Film Depictions of the Crusades and Christian-Muslim*

Clashes. eds. Nickolas Haydock and E.L. Risden. Jefferson, NC: McFarland, 2009, pp. 97–122.

Sturtevant, Paul B. 'Kingdom of Heaven's Road Map for Peace'. *Bulletin of International Medieval Research* 12 (2006), pp. 23–40.

———. 'SaladiNasser: Nasser's Political Crusade in *El Naser Salah Ad-Din*'. In *Hollywood in the Holy Land: Essays on Film Depictions of the Crusades and Christian-Muslim Clashes*. eds. Nickolas Haydock and E.L. Risden. Jefferson, NC: McFarland, 2009, pp. 123–46.

Tyerman, Christopher. *The Debate on the Crusades, 1099–2010*. Manchester: MUP, 2011.

———. *God's War: A New History of the Crusades*. Cambridge, MA: Belknap Press, 2006.

———. 'Were There Any Crusades in the Twelfth Century?' In *The Invention of the Crusades*. ed. Christopher Tyerman. Toronto: University of Toronto Press, 1998, pp. 8–29.

4 'The Evil Genius of the Third Crusade'

Conrad of Montferrat, stereotype and scapegoat

Marianne McLeod Gilchrist

Ara sai eu de pretz quals l'a plus gran ('Now I know whose is the greatest worth') wrote Bertran de Born, praising Conrad of Montferrat's defence of Tyre (1187–90), and berating Philip II of France (r. 1180–1223) and Richard I of England (r. 1189–99) for delaying going to his aid.[1] Anglophone popular histories and fiction, however, more often depict Conrad as a treacherous villain. The English historian William Stubbs dubbed Conrad 'the evil genius of the Third Crusade'[2] and blamed him for his own death: 'it is a wonder he was not disposed of earlier than he was'.[3] Steven Runciman made him a fugitive killer.[4] He could as easily have become the Third Crusade's tragic hero: brilliant, brave, and handsome, according to Niketas Choniates; with a talent for turning up in time to resolve crises; elected king, but assassinated before his coronation.[5] The historian Charles Mills had portrayed him positively, writing of his election as king: 'The imbecile Guy had but few partisans, and the public voice was in favour of the valiant Conrad.'[6] However, popular works, including films, which treat the Third Crusade as 'Richard versus Saladin', outweighed this possibility with a hostile tradition. Here I will explore some of the most influential examples.

Literary framing

Conrad's vilification in post-medieval Anglophone writings stemmed from the succession dispute after Queen Sibyl of Jerusalem (r. 1186–90) and her daughters died at Acre in 1190. Guy of Lusignan, her widower, sought to remain king, but Conrad, marrying her half-sister Isabel (r. 1190–1205), was supported by the local nobility and his kinsman Philip of France. The Anglo-Angevin *Itinerarium Peregrinorum* and works of Ambroise and Roger of Howden reflected Richard I's support for Guy and claim to crusade leadership. Rejecting the legality of Conrad's marriage and thus his kingship,[7] they denounced him for negotiating directly with Saladin. This enabled *The Crusade and Death of Richard I*, based on Roger, and the fourteenth-century English romance *Richard Coer de Lyon* to depict him as a 'traitor' in Saladin's pay.[8]

Having acquired some of Raymond III of Tripoli's former allies, Conrad was linked retrospectively to Raymond's alleged treachery *before* the battle of Hattin (1187). That he arrived in Tyre only *after* Hattin was ignored: a Marquis of Montferrat – his father, William – had been there. The *Narratives of the Minstrel of Reims* (1260s–90s)[9] and a related romance, *Le Pas Saladin*, elided them.[10] This composite marquis re-emerged in the popular computer game *Assassin's Creed* (2007), named 'William' because it was set in 1191, when the father died.

Returning from the crusade, Richard was arrested by Meinhard II of Gorizia (Conrad's nephew) for plotting Conrad's assassination and handed over to Leopold V of Austria (his second cousin, r. 1177–94). The murder accusation against Richard was dismissed. Novelist George Alfred Henty in 1882 claimed Richard had 'appointed' Conrad king as a conciliatory gesture.[11] In *For Cross or Crescent*, William Stables condemned Conrad as 'a bully, and treacherous to a degree', having Richard say: 'I […] was accused of causing the death of the Marquis of Montferret [sic], not a hair of whose head I could have had the heart to injure.'[12] Lawrence du Garde Peach's Ladybird children's educational book, *Richard the Lionheart* (1965), described the Blondel legend as 'not true', but omitted Conrad entirely and depicted Richard's imprisonment as Leopold's 'revenge for the insult to his flag' at Acre.[13]

Walter Scott made the flag dispute central to *The Talisman* (1825) but changed its context. This novel, on which generations of future historians and writers grew up, created the dominant template for crusade fiction and depictions of Conrad.[14] Eleanor Porden's verse-epic, *Cœur de Lion* (1822), had more historical content, though romanticised, with Conrad a swashbuckling Byronic rogue whose half-crazed Byzantine wife interrupted his wedding to Isabel.[15] While it possibly influenced *Jane Eyre*, it could not match Scott's international reach: five editions of his works were published in Milan in 1830 alone.[16] Translations of *The Talisman*, often retitled *Riccardo Cuor di Leone*, appeared throughout the twentieth century, including Fabbri's illustrated children's abridged versions (1969–70).

Enlightenment historiography led Scott to depict Saladin as the Franks' moral superior; his villains therefore had to be Frankish.[17] As Mills had noted of *Ivanhoe* (1819), 'when he wants a villain […] he as regularly and unscrupulously resorts to the fraternity of the Templars as other novelists refer to the church, or to Italy.'[18] In *The Talisman*, Scott used both. He invented a conspiracy against Richard by Grand Master Giles Amaury (a fictional substitute for Guy's ally Gerard of Rideford and Richard's placeman

Robert de Sablé), with Conrad as his henchman. He combined the treacherous Marquis of Montferrat from the *Richard Coer de Lyon* romance (which he knew)[19] with Italian ethnic stereotypes from contemporary Gothic novels – the scheming Machiavellian and dandified, unctuous *cicisbeo*. Misreading 'f' as 'long s' in printed sources, he turned Montferrat into 'Montserrat', redesigning Conrad's blazon as 'a serrated and rocky mountain'.[20] Scott made *Conrad* attack *Richard*'s banner, injuring Roswal, the Scots hero Sir Kenneth's hound. In trial by combat, Kenneth wounded Conrad, whom the Grand Master then stabbed to prevent him confessing. Since a dwarf jester witnessed the murder, Saladin beheaded the Grand Master: a scene derived from Reynald of Châtillon's killing after Hattin.

In *The Life and Death of Richard Yea-and-Nay* (1900), Maurice Hewlett portrayed Conrad as a usurper, ignoring his ties to the kingdom through his brother William Longsword and nephew Baldwin V. Conrad was said to have 'the ravished wife of old King Baldwin for title-deed',[21] with Richard saying: 'I will never get a kingdom for him, and I marvel that King Philip can make no better choice than of a man whose only title is rape'.[22] Hewlett conflated Baldwin III's widow, Theodora Komnene (who eloped with Andronikos Komnenos) with Conrad's second wife, Theodora Angelina, and Queen Isabel. This 'rape' claim may have inspired his most extreme 'Gothic villain' depiction in the American edition of Graham Shelby's *The Kings of Vain Intent* (1970): 'the monster of Montferrat', who flogs and rapes Isabel.[23] Hewlett placed Conrad at the French court in 1188–9, rather than defending Tyre. His Conrad schemed with Philip II and Richard's brother John: 'any king of England who would help him to the throne of Jerusalem was the king of England he would serve.'[24] He then accompanied Richard and Philip on crusade in 1190. There, his plot to have Richard killed by the Assassins was discovered by Jehane, Richard's fictional mistress.[25] She persuaded their leader, Sinan, to prevent the murder in exchange for marrying him.[26] When Conrad arrived, Sinan ordered two Assassins: 'Return with the Marquess to the coast by the way of Emesa and Baalbek; and when you are within sight of Sidon, strike. One of you will be burned alive. [...] Let the other return speedily with a token [...].'[27] That 'token' was Conrad's severed hand. Hewlett later had Jehane carry Sinan's letters to Europe to clear Richard's name. In 1199 Sinan let her join Richard in France – without telling her he had sent Assassins to kill the king. Reconciled with the dying Richard, she admitted her role in Conrad's murder: 'He deserved it.'[28]

Hewlett's key innovation, which informed Conrad's portrayal in Cecil B. DeMille's *The Crusades* (1935), was depicting him conspiring against Richard *in Europe* and plotting *his* assassination. To absolve Richard fully, Conrad had to be shown as a murderer or attempted murderer himself – to merit his own death. Similarly, in *A History of the Crusades* (1952),

Runciman decided to depict him fleeing to Tyre after being 'involved in a murder' in Constantinople.[29] That 'murder' was his defeat of Vranas in battle, described in Niketas Choniates' *Historia*,[30] yet Runciman, one of the few popular Western writers familiar with Choniates, misrepresented it.

Playing the villain on stage and screen

Conrad had appeared on stage sympathetically in Italy in Francesco Ottavio Magnocavallo's neo-classical tragedy *Corrado, Marchese di Monferrato* (1772), but adaptations of *The Talisman* dominated the nineteenth century. Many were operas or musical productions: *The Knights of the Cross, or The Hermit's Prophecy* (1826), by Beazley and Bishop; *Il Talismano; ossia, la Terza Crociata in Palestina* (1829), by Barbieri and Pacini, which premiered in 1829 in Naples and was performed in Milan and, in 1835, in Viareggio[31]; *Richard en Palestine* (1844), by Foucher and Adam; and *Il Talismano* (1874), by Matthison and Balfe. Pacini's *Il Talismano* elided Conrad with Leopold and the Grand Master into one villain, while Balfe focused on young lovers Edith and Kenneth. Beazley and Bishop had Conrad wounded in the judicial combat but *not* murdered afterwards. Julius Benedict and Alfred Bunn's 1846 opera *The Crusaders* (*Der Alte vom Berge* in German) began with the assassination of King Conrade of Jerusalem, but progressed with more influence from Tasso's *Gerusalemme Liberata*.[32] Nino Berrini's *Rambaldo di Vaqueiras* (*I Monferrato*) (1922), modelled on Edmond Rostand's *La Princesse Lointaine* and *Cyrano de Bergerac*, featured Conrad as a sympathetic minor character. It could not compete with Scott-based films, the earliest of which, *Richard the Lion-hearted* (Chester 'Chet' Withey, 1923), showed Kenneth rescuing Edith 'from the unholy power of Conrad, and Richard fights Saladin in a spirited combat out of which comes a treaty of peace and fellowship'.[33]

During the Cold War, *The Talisman*'s focus on traitors undermining the crusade from within paralleled fears of Communist infiltration. The Arthurian adventure film *The Black Knight* (1954), loosely based on the romance of Gareth and Linet, starring Alan Ladd, had a similar emphasis.[34] *King Richard and the Crusaders* (David Butler, 1954), scripted by John Twist, starred Rex Harrison as Saladin and George Sanders as Richard. The 1930 Motion Picture Production Code ('Hays Code'), prohibited villainous or comic depictions of clergy, so the Templars were renamed the 'Knights of Castle Refuge', 'Castelaines', or 'Castlers': *Ivanhoe* (1952) similarly excised Templar references.[35]

In *The Talisman*, Scott anachronistically introduced Conrad's brother 'Enguerrand' (*sic*, for Boniface) as a Venetian ally.[36] In Butler's film, Philip of France described Conrad (Michael Pate) as 'the wise Venetian whose gold pays for much of this crusade'. He threatened to withdraw this unless the Grand Master was appointed commander. He was shown knifing a guard in the back and poisoning the arrow used to shoot Richard – embodying precisely the racist Gothic stereotype John Chetwode Eustace had denounced in 1815 of the 'Italian [...] with a dose of poison in one hand and a dagger in the other'.[37] His portrayal as a Venetian moneylender evoked another dubious stereotype – Shylock in *The Merchant of Venice*. In the film, Sir Kenneth (Laurence Harvey) killed him in a swordfight immediately after the hound Roswal recognised him.

On television, *Richard the Lionheart* (Ernest Morris, ITV, 1962–3) borrowed freely from *The Talisman* in the episode 'A Marriage of Convenience' (1962), in which Conrad (Michael Peake), not Richard (Dermot Walsh), plotted Edith's marriage to Saladin.[38] BBC1's *The Talisman* (Richard Bramall, 1980–1), with Damien Thomas as Saladin and Richard Morant as Conrad, and a two-part Russian version (1992–3), *Rytsar Kennet* ('Sir Kenneth') and *Richard lvinoe serdtse* ('Richard the Lionheart'), were more faithful. The *Doctor Who* adventure 'The Crusade' (BBC1, 1965), by David Whitaker, restored Joanna of Sicily and 'Saphadin' (Al-Adil), Saladin's brother, to their historical roles in Richard's marriage diplomacy. The series initially had educational aspirations, but the 'historical' adventures owed more to popular fiction: for example, *Reign of Terror* (1963) drew on Emmuska Orczy's *Scarlet Pimpernel* novels.[39] *The Crusade* adhered to Scott's focus on romance tropes: Barbara's abduction into a harem, Richard knighting Ian, and Vicki's disguise as a youth.[40] Richard and Saladin were treated favourably, while the villains were fictional. 'Conrad of Tyre', though mentioned, remained off-screen. Instead, his fictional envoy, Luigi Ferrigo (Gábor Baraker), a Genoese merchant, replaced not only Reynald Grenier but – as a stereotyped scheming Italian – Conrad himself: his surname, 'Ferrigo', echoing 'Monferrato'. Saladin, whose fictional role from *The Talisman* onward included exposing Frankish traitors, uncovered Luigi's involvement in Barbara's abduction.

Cecil B. DeMille's *The Crusades* (1935) gave Conrad his most prominent screen portrayal. It was a typical DeMille fable: the boorish Richard (Henry Wilcoxon) discovering true faith through love for the devout Berengaria (Loretta Young) and chivalric encounters with Saladin (Ian Keith). Saladin's portrayal was drawn from *The Talisman*, including his slicing silk to show off his superior sword.[41] His idealisation as leader of 'highly civilized and chivalrous foemen' meant DeMille, like Scott, had to find an enemy among the Franks, where he divined 'motives ranging from the purest faith to the blackest treachery and greed'.[42] He chose Conrad.[43] The sources credited on-screen were Harold Lamb's popular histories, *Iron Men and Saints* and *The Flame of Islam* (1930). Despite repeating Scott's

'Montserrat' error, Lamb wrote of Conrad: 'Baha ad Din says he was a great personage, wise and energetic, and other Moslems [...] call him worse than a wolf and meaner than a dog. He had firm friends and bitter enemies.'[44] Lamb wrote the film's song lyrics, but his script contribution is unclear. Conrad's portrayal drew more strongly on *The Life and Death of Richard Yea-and-Nay* – unacknowledged, as it was still in copyright.

Following Hewlett, the script placed Conrad in Europe in 1187–90, conspiring with Philip of France and Prince John to arrange Richard's death on crusade and make him King of Jerusalem. Joseph Schildkraut, whom DeMille had cast as Judas (*King of Kings*, 1927) and Herod (*Cleopatra*, 1934), played Conrad as a Machiavellian schemer, slighter than Hewlett's 'large, pale, ruminating Italian',[45] his costume suggestive of Shakespeare's *Richard III*. Toying with a dagger, he assured John: 'I have the direst premonition tonight that your lion-hearted brother will never return to England. In fact, I can give you my word for it.' His blazon, changed to *party per chevron, in base a serpent*, emphasised his venomous slipperiness.

In the camp at Acre, Conrad convinced Berengaria she was to blame for hostility between Richard and Philip, driving her to place herself in the line of fire. Wounded, she was rescued by Saladin and became a Hays Code-friendly surrogate for Hewlett's Jehane in revealing Conrad's treachery. When Conrad arrived in Saladin's camp, the guards disarmed him:

Saladin: What brings Conrad of Montferrat to me?
Conrad: I offer you victory.
Saladin: Tomorrow I shall win it: the crusade is broken.
Conrad: Not yet. Victory is not sure while Richard of England lives.
Saladin: You're his brother's friend.
Conrad: And would be yours.
Saladin: What price do you ask for your treachery?
Conrad: The Kingdom of Jerusalem, which I shall rule under you.
Saladin: And what do you offer me?
Conrad: Richard's death. Within the hour, he will lie on the battlefield among the slain.
Saladin: Who would slay your lion of the crusaders?
Conrad: Fifteen swords of mine follow him where he goes alone. With Richard dead, you will rule unchallenged in Asia.
Saladin: I have no traffic with assassins. Away with this dog!

The guards killed him off-screen, with audible screams. After defeating an attack by Conrad's men, Richard was reconciled with Berengaria and, at her instigation, made peace.

Maud Hughes, in *Picture Show*, warned: 'people who respect history will have reason to be annoyed at de Mille's [sic] garbled version of the story'.[46]

TIME called it 'historically worthless, didactically treacherous, artistically absurd'.[47] Like Scott, DeMille admitted 'telescoping history': 'Audiences are not interested in dates: they are interested in events and their meaning. We chose the year 1187 as the focal point for our story, but did not hesitate to bring in elements from other Crusades before or after that exact time.'[48] Despite initial losses, *The Crusades* was re-released in 1951. This screening probably influenced Ronald Welch's children's novel, *Knight Crusader* (1954), in which the description of Conrad resembled Schildkraut's: 'a sleek cat of a man, olive of complexion, and long of face, with white, fluttering hands, and a silky voice'.[49] As recently as 2004, Anton Kozlovic defended DeMille's 'dastardly' depiction of Conrad, claiming he 'historically, was an unsavoury character'[50] – based on Karen Armstrong's uncritical repetition of Runciman's murder allegation.[51]

In 1954, when DeMille and Wilcoxon filmed *The Ten Commandments* in Egypt, General Abdel Hakim Amer, Minister of War, told them:

> The Crusades was a very popular film in our Muslim country – due to its fair presentation of both sides and its portrayal of Saladin as a great and holy leader of his people. So popular, in fact, that it ran for three years in the same theater. And during those three years, when Colonel Nasser and I were first in military academy, we saw The Crusades perhaps as many as twenty times. It was our favorite picture. […] Colonel Nasser was so taken with the character of the Lionheart in your movie that he told everyone in the military academy that when he grew up he was going to be just like that, and that's how the other boys came to call him Henry Wilcoxon![52]

Gamal Abdel Nasser had overthrown Egypt's monarchy in 1952, defeated Britain and France in the 1956 Suez Crisis, and, like Saladin, united Egypt and Syria (United Arab Republic) from 1958 to 1961. Youssef Chahine's *Saladin the Victorious* (*El Naser Salah Ad-Din*) (1963), punning on Nasser's name, projected his secular pan-Arab nationalism back in time. The opening scenes of oppressed Arabs represented not only pre-Nasser Egypt, but also Algeria and Palestine. There was no acknowledgement that Saladin was a Kurd, not an Arab.

Chahine, of Melkite Catholic background, knew Scott's *The Talisman* and *Ivanhoe* from his British-style education at Alexandria's Victoria College, and DeMille's film. As John Aberth pointed out, his depiction of the siege of Acre as 'a picnic', resolved through the governor's treachery, was taken from the First Crusade siege of Antioch, in DeMille-style 'telescoping'.[53] Just as Scott and Hollywood elevated Saladin as the noble opponent, so Chahine idealised Richard alone of the Frankish leaders. He even exonerated Richard for massacring prisoners from the Acre garrison.

Instead, he showed Philip (who in reality had already set off home) ordering it, perhaps reflecting anti-French sentiments over the Algerian War of Independence, the subject of his earlier film, *Jamila the Algerian* (*Jamila al-Jaza'iriyya*) (1958).

Chahine made Conrad (Mahmoud El-Meliguy) a lover of Virginia of Kerak (Leila Fawzi): as Reynald of Châtillon's widow and would-be queen, she served as a composite fictional substitute for Stephanie of Milly, Sibyl, and Isabel. At Virginia's urging, Conrad conspired against Richard and the fictional heroine Louise of Lusignan, a Tasso-esque female Knight Hospitaller. Louise turned against the crusade through love for an Arab Christian, Issa, so Conrad and Virginia had her tried for treason: a scene echoing Rebecca's trial in *Ivanhoe*. A split screen juxtaposed Louise's unjust trial with Saladin's fair trial of the Governor of Acre, whom Virginia had seduced. Richard, seeing through Conrad's deceit, instead ordered *his* beheading. Virginia next beguiled Richard's fictional advisor, Arthur, with whom she plotted the king's death by poisoned arrow, as in *King Richard and the Crusaders*. However, as in Butler's film and its source, *The Talisman*, Saladin healed Richard. Arthur strangled Virginia when, wounded in battle, she confessed to Louise – echoing the Grand Master killing the wounded Conrad in *The Talisman*. The film ended with Richard making peace with Saladin and entering Jerusalem (for a second time) as a pilgrim, Arthur becoming insane, and Louise marrying Issa.

Sir Ridley: heir to Sir Walter?

Like the Cold War swashbucklers and *Saladin the Victorious*, Ridley Scott's *Kingdom of Heaven* (2005) reflected contemporary politics, conceived in New York in November 2001 after the 11 September terrorist attacks.[54] It was set in 1184–7, culminating in the siege of Jerusalem, with an epilogue *c.* 1190. The 'enemy within' this time embodied religious fanaticism: 'leaders who try to make peace are admired, but their efforts so often are subverted by more radical factions'.[55] As in *The Talisman*, the Templars were assigned this role, 'the right wing or Christian fundamentalists of their day'.[56] Despite the leading role of his ally Balian of Ibelin, Conrad was absent, as were Isabel and her mother, Maria Komnene – the historical Balian's wife. Sibyl – here 'Sibylla', as in Runciman – was the only significant female character, conflated with Isabel, who had appeared briefly in an early draft.

William Monahan had wanted to write a historical script, inspired by boyhood reading of Runciman: 'Baldwin IV, the idea of him in a silver mask, had haunted me since I was fourteen or so.'[57] Scott's initial concept, mentioned in his DVD commentary, was of a blacksmith becoming a knight, suggesting youthful memories of Alan Ladd as John the Blacksmith in the

Cold War Arthurian swashbuckler *The Black Knight* (1954). These concepts did not dovetail easily. Scott and Monahan claimed to use primary sources,[58] following James Reston's plagiarism allegations over *Warriors of God*,[59] but seemed unaware of any post-Runciman scholarship. Scott insisted: 'The way to get over the controversy is to try to be accurate and to try to tell the truth,'[60] and the film was marketed as 'truthful', telling the story 'as accurately as possible'.[61] However, Jonathan Riley-Smith observed: 'where they could have created fictional characters they have opted for real historical personalities whom they have distorted ruthlessly. The characters and careers of the hero, his lover, her husband, the king and Saladin have been re-manufactured to suit the needs of the script.'[62]

Aside from his defence of Jerusalem, Scott's Balian (Orlando Bloom) bore scant resemblance to his historical namesake, being a bastard-born French smith, who fled to take up his father's fief after killing his half-brother, a corrupt priest. Scott asserted disingenuously: 'Sure, there is no evidence that Balian was ever a blacksmith – but there's no evidence to say he wasn't.'[63] He became a military engineering expert for Baldwin IV (Edward Norton) and lover of Sibylla (Eva Green), herself unhappily married to Guy (Marton Csokas). In the Director's Cut she poisoned her son (Conrad's nephew), Baldwin V, after discovering his leprosy – a fiction, but Scott's commentary suggests he came to believe it, with other fabrications such as Reynald of Châtillon murdering Saladin's sister.

Ridley Scott was indebted to his namesake Walter's model of historical fiction and (via Monahan) Runciman's novelistic history. Like Runciman, in Tyerman's words, he appealed to 'the sense that people in the past were essentially just like people in the present; and that […] the past can be judged according to hindsight and modern schemes of value, ethics and morality'.[64] Denying that 'the medieval mind was very different to ours',[65] his sympathetic characters were twenty-first-century figures in fancy dress: 'Balian is an agnostic, just like me,' he claimed.[66] As Riley-Smith responded succinctly to early reports of the film: 'It sounds absolute balls.'[67]

However, in presenting Balian as the gifted incomer defending the kingdom and winning a princess from an unworthy husband, Scott and Monahan made him a partial surrogate for Conrad. They depicted him as a fugitive murderer, as Runciman had Conrad,[68] but in reality more like the Lusignans, banished from Poitou for killing Patrick, Earl of Salisbury.[69] Stubbs had contrasted Guy, whose defeat at Hattin almost destroyed the kingdom, 'a brave soldier, a good commander, an honourable and generous enemy, and faithful friend', with Conrad: 'ruthless in enmity, faithless in friendship, cunning and unscrupulous enough to pass for an Italian of a later age'.[70] *Kingdom of Heaven* overturned this. Scott pressed Monahan to make Guy 'more of an autonomous villain rather than the confused and easily led man described by his contemporaries'.[71] In an early draft, Guy stabbed Isabel's first husband, Humphrey of Toron, and was beheaded by Balian in a swordfight.[72] While Stubbs, like Walter Scott, had been anti-Italian, Ridley Scott associated Guy's Frenchness with snobbish 'Old World' privilege, with his sneer at Balian: 'In France, *this* could not inherit.' Scott had no place for a hero who strove for kingship and its responsibilities. Film-Balian told Sibylla: 'Decide not to be a queen, and I will come to you,' and – unlike his historical counterpart – he fled the country after surrendering Jerusalem.

What would Stubbs have made of his chivalrous Guy replacing Conrad as the 'evil genius'? He accepted uncritically Conrad of Montferrat's villainous presentation in the Anglo-Angevin texts he edited, in a culture where Walter Scott was as ubiquitous as Ridley Scott today. All historians grow up and live among historical novels, films, and now computer games. If these collectively and cumulatively reinforce one interpretation, transcending it takes effort. Conrad's treatment shows the arbitrariness of many 'hero' and 'villain' labels, rooted in nationalistic narratives and ethnic stereotyping. They are combatted not by merely reversing them (as in Ridley Scott's vilification of Guy of Lusignan), but by leaving them behind.

Notes

1 Bertran de Born, *The Poems of the Troubadour Bertran de Born*, eds. William D. Paden Jr., Tilde Sankovitch, and Patricia H. Stäblein (Berkeley, 1986), Song 41, pp. 414–21.
2 Roger of Howden, *Chronica Magistri Rogeri de Houeden*, ed. William Stubbs, vol. 2 (London, 1868–71), p. 194, n. 3.
3 William Stubbs, ed., *Itinerarium Peregrinorum et Gesta Regis Ricardi* (London, 1864), pp. xxii–iv.
4 Runciman, *Crusades*, 2, p. 384; Marianne McLeod Gilchrist, 'Getting away with Murder: Runciman and Conrad of Montferrat's Career in Constantinople', *The Mediæval Journal* 2:1 (2012), pp. 15–36.
5 Niketas Choniates, *Nicetae Choniatae Historia*, ed. Jan-Louis van Dieten, vol. 1 (Berlin, 1975), p. 201.
6 Charles Mills, *The History of the Crusades*, vol. 2 (London, 1822), p. 62.
7 See Gilchrist, 'Getting Away', pp. 21–3.
8 Ronald C. Johnston, ed., *The Crusade and Death of Richard I* (Oxford, 1961), p. 28; Karl Brunner, ed., *Der Mittelenglische Versroman über Richard Löwenherz* (Vienna, 1913), pp. 228–9, 257–8.
9 Natalis de Wailly, ed., *Récits d'un Ménestrel de Reims au Treizième Siècle* (Paris, 1876), p. 14; for dating, pp. xxx–xxxiv.
10 Gaston Paris, 'La Légende de Saladin: quatrième et dernier article', *Journal des Savants* (1893), p. 487.
11 George Alfred Henty, *Winning His Spurs* (London, 1882), pp. 182, 209.
12 William Gordon Stables, *For Cross or Crescent* (London: 1897), pp. 351, 347.

13 Lawrence du Garde Peach, *Richard the Lionheart* (Loughborough, 1965), pp. 30–2.
14 See Gilchrist, 'Getting Away', pp. 15–36; Marianne McLeod Gilchrist, 'Bleedthrough: The Two-Way Traffic between Popular Historiography and Fiction', *Journal of Historical Fictions* 2:1 (April 2019), pp. 18–25.
15 Eleanor Anne Porden, *Cœur de Lion*, vol. 1 (London, 1822), pp. 179–82.
16 Siberry, *New Crusaders*, p. 124.
17 Robert Irwin, 'Saladin and the Third Crusade: A Case Study in Historiography and the Historical Novel' in *A Companion to Historiography*, ed. Michael Bentley (London, 1997), pp. 140–3; Gilchrist, 'Getting Away', pp. 32–3.
18 Charles Mills, *The History of Chivalry*, vol. 1 (London, 1825), pp. 337–8.
19 Jerome Mitchell, *Scott, Chaucer, and Medieval Romance* (Lexington, KY, 1987), pp. 19–20.
20 Walter Scott, *The Talisman*, (Oxford, 1912), p. 331.
21 Maurice Hewlett, *The Life and Death of Richard Yea-and-Nay* (London, 1900), p. 238.
22 Ibid., p. 209.
23 Graham Shelby, *The Kings of Vain Intent* (New York, 1970), pp. 190, 105–7.
24 Hewlett, *Richard Yea-and-Nay*, p. 149.
25 Ibid., pp. 298–9.
26 Ibid., p. 314–17.
27 Ibid., p. 322.
28 Ibid., p. 423.
29 Runciman, *Crusades*, 2, p. 384.
30 Choniates, *Historia*, 1, pp. 386–7; Gilchrist, 'Getting Away', pp. 19–20.
31 Jerome Mitchell, *The Walter Scott Operas* (Tuscaloosa, AL, 1977), p. 305.
32 See ibid., pp. 301–26, and Siberry, *The New Crusaders*, p. 176.
33 Henry Adalbert White, *Sir Walter Scott's Novels on the Stage* (New Haven, CT, 1927), p. 184, citing studio publicity materials.
34 See John Aberth, *A Knight at the Movies* (London, 2003), pp. 11–16.
35 Jeffrey Richards, 'Sir Ridley Scott and the Rebirth of the Historical Epic' in *The Return of the Epic Film*, ed. Andrew B.R. Elliott (Edinburgh, 2013), pp. 29–30.
36 Scott, *Talisman*, p. 365.
37 See Kenneth Churchill, *Italy and English Literature 1764–1930* (London, 1980), p. 19.
38 Tise Vahimagi, 'Richard the Lionheart (1961–65)', *BFI: Screenonline*, British Film Institute, London <http://www.screenonline.org.uk/tv/id/1136160/synopsis.html>, [accessed 25 September 2019].
39 See Gilchrist, 'Bleedthrough', p. 28.
40 See David Whitaker, *Doctor Who and the Crusaders* (London, 1965), and online photonovel, <http://www.bbc.co.uk/doctorwho/classic/photonovels/crusade>, [accessed 8 September 2019].
41 Cecil B. DeMille, *The Autobiography of Cecil B. DeMille*, ed. Donald Hayne (Englewood Cliffs, NJ, 1959), p. 313; Scott, *Talisman*, pp. 419–21.
42 DeMille, *Autobiography*, p. 344.
43 Gerald E. Forshey, *American Religious and Biblical Spectaculars* (Westport, CT, 1992), p. 19.
44 Harold Lamb, *The Flame of Islam* (New York, 1930), p. 99.
45 Hewlett, *Richard Yea-and-Nay*, p. 82.
46 Maud Hughes, 'Big Pictures of 1935: *The Crusades*', *Picture Show*, 21 September 1935, p. 9.

47 Anonymous review, 'The New Pictures', *TIME*, 2 September 1935, <http://www.time.com/time/magazine/article/0,9171,755038,00.html>, [accessed 28 September 2019].
48 DeMille, *Autobiography*, p. 344.
49 Ronald Welch, *Knight Crusader* (Oxford, 1954), p. 189.
50 Anton Karl Kozlovic, 'The Deep Focus Typecasting of Joseph Schildkraut as Judas Figure in Four DeMille Films', Journal of Religion and Popular Culture 6 (Spring 2004), paras 71–76, <https://dspace.flinders.edu.au/xmlui/handle/2328/14270>, [accessed 29 September 2019].
51 Karen Armstrong, *Holy War* (London, 1992), pp. xi, 255.
52 Henry Wilcoxon and Katherine Orrison, *Lionheart in Hollywood* (Metuchen, NJ, 1991), pp. 274–5; DeMille, *Autobiography*, p. 386.
53 Aberth, *Knight at the Movies*, pp. 91–107.
54 Diana Landau, ed., *Kingdom of Heaven* (London, 2005), pp. 24–5, 47.
55 Ridley Scott, in ibid., p. 8.
56 Ibid., p. 11.
57 Ibid., p. 47.
58 Ibid., pp. 48–50.
59 Dalya Alberge, 'Ridley Scott Denies Plagiarism in Crusades Movie', *Times*, 31 March 2005, <https://www.thetimes.co.uk/article/ridley-scott-denies-plagiarism-in-crusades-movie-n8djntb9kq7>, [accessed 23 September 2019].
60 Garth Pearce, 'Great Scott Ridley Packs a Punch', *Times*, 17 April 2005, <https://www.thetimes.co.uk/article/great-scott-ridley-packs-a-punch-cwb7f7nbxbl> [accessed 22 September 2019].
61 Leaflet insert, *Kingdom of Heaven: 4-Disc Director's Cut* (2006).
62 Jonathan Riley-Smith, 'Truth Is the First Victim', *Times*, 5 May 2005, <https://www.thetimes.co.uk/article/truth-is-the-first-victim-p9zsd2d7nsb>, [accessed 22 September 2019].
63 Pearce, 'Great Scott Ridley'.
64 Christopher Tyerman, *The Debate on the Crusades* (Manchester, 2011), p. 199.
65 Ridley Scott, in Landau, *Kingdom of Heaven*, p. 10.
66 Pearce, 'Great Scott Ridley'.
67 Charlotte Edwardes, 'Ridley Scott's New Crusades Film "Panders to Osama bin Laden"', *Telegraph*, 18 January 2004, <https://www.telegraph.co.uk/news/worldnews/northamerica/usa/1452000/Ridley-Scotts-new-Crusades-film-panders-to-Osama-bin-Laden.html>, [accessed 22 September 2019].
68 Runciman, *Crusades*, 2, p. 384; Gilchrist, 'Getting Away', pp. 15–36.
69 Roger of Howden, *Chronica*, 1, pp. 273–4; Gilchrist, 'Getting Away', pp. 30–1.
70 Stubbs, *Itinerarium Peregrinorum*, pp. cxxiv–v.
71 Landau, *Kingdom of Heaven*, p. 51.
72 William Monahan, *Kingdom of Heaven*, undated draft script, *c.* 2002, pp. 122, 150.

Bibliography

Primary

Alberge, Dalya. 'Ridley Scott denies plagiarism in Crusades movie.' *Times*, 31 March 2005. www.thetimes.co.uk/article/ridley-scott-denies-plagiarism-in-crusades-movie-n8djntb9kq7. [Accessed 23 September 2019].

Anonymous. 'The New Pictures'. *TIME*, 2 September 1935. www.time.com/time/magazine/article/0,9171,755038,00.html. [Accessed 28 September 2019].

Bertran de Born. *The Poems of the Troubadour Bertran de Born*. Eds. William D. Paden Jr., Tilde Sankovitch, and Patricia H. Stäblein. Berkeley, CA: University of California Press, 1986.

Brunner, Karl. ed. *Der Mittelenglische Versroman über Richard Löwenherz. Wiener Beitrage zur Englischen Philologie*. Vol. 42. Vienna: Wilhelm Braumüller, 1913.

Choniates, Niketas. *Nicetae Choniatae Historia*. Ed. Jan-Louis van Dieten. *Corpus Fontium Historiae Byzantinae* 11. Berlin: Walter de Gruyter, 1975.

de Wailly, Natalis, ed. *Récits d'un Ménestrel de Reims au Treizième Siècle*. Paris: Societé de l'Histoire de France, 1876.

Edwardes, Charlotte. 'Ridley Scott's new crusades film "panders to Osama bin Laden"'. *The Telegraph*, 18 January 2004. www.telegraph.co.uk/news/world news/northamerica/usa/1452000/Ridley-Scotts-new-Crusades-film-panders-to-Osama-bin-Laden.html. [Accessed 22 September 2019].

Henty, George Alfred. *Winning His Spurs: A Tale of the Crusades*. London: Sampson Low, Marston, Searle and Rivington, 1882.

Hewlett, Maurice. *The Life and Death of Richard Yea-and-Nay*. London and New York: Macmillan, 1900.

Hughes, Maud. 'Big Pictures of 1935: *The Crusades*'. *Picture Show*, 21 September 1935, p. 9.

Johnston, Ronald Carlyle, ed. *The Crusade and Death of Richard I. Anglo-Norman Texts*. Vol. 17. Oxford: OUP, 1961.

Landau, Diane. ed. *Kingdom of Heaven: The Ridley Scott Film and the History Behind the Story*. London: Simon & Schuster, 2005.

Monahan, William. *Kingdom of Heaven*. Undated script draft in typescript. *c.* 2002.

Paris, Gaston. 'La Légende de Saladin: quatrième et dernier article'. *Journal des Savants* (1893), pp. 486–98.

Peach, Lawrence du Garde. *Richard the Lionheart: An Adventure from History*. Loughborough: Wills & Hepworth, 1965.

Pearce, Garth. 'Great Scott Ridley packs a punch'. *Times*, 17 April 2005. www.thetimes.co.uk/article/great-scott-ridley-packs-a-punch-cwb7f7nbxbl. [Accessed 22 September 2019].

Porden, Eleanor Anne. *Cœur de Lion; or The Third Crusade*. London: G. & W.B. Whittaker, 1822.

Riley-Smith, Jonathan. 'Truth is the first victim'. *Times*, 5 May 2005. www.thetimes.co.uk/article/truth-is-the-first-victim-p9zsd2d7nsb. [Accessed 22 September 2019].

Roger of Howden. *Chronica Magistri Rogeri de Houeden*. Ed. William Stubbs. Rolls Series 51. London: Longmans, Green and Co, 1868–71.

Scott, Walter. *The Talisman*. Oxford: OUP, 1912.

Shelby, Graham. *The Kings of Vain Intent*. New York: Weybright and Talley, 1970.

Stables, William Gordon. *For Cross or Crescent: The Days of Richard the Lionhearted*. London: Dean, 1897.

Stubbs, William, ed. *Itinerarium Peregrinorum et Gesta Regis Ricardi*, Rolls Series 38. London: Longman, Green, Longman, Roberts and Green, 1864.

Welch, Ronald. *Knight Crusader*. Oxford: OUP, 1954.
Whitaker, David. *Doctor Who and the Crusaders*. London: Frederick Muller, 1965.

Secondary

Aberth, John. *A Knight at the Movies: Medieval History on Film*. London and New York: Routledge, 2003.
Armstrong, Karen. *Holy War: The Crusades and Their Impact on Today's World*. London: Macmillan, 1988, updated edition, 1992.
Burt, Richard. 'Cutting and (Re)Running from the (Medieval) Middle East: The Return of the Film Epic and the Uncanny Mise-hors-scènes of *Kingdom of Heaven*'s Double DVDs'. In *Medieval and Early Modern Film and Media*. ed. Richard Burt. Houndmills and New York: Palgrave Macmillan, 2008, pp. 107–36.
Churchill, Kenneth. *Italy and English Literature 1764–1930*. London: Macmillan, 1980.
DeMille, Cecil B. *The Autobiography of Cecil B. DeMille*. Ed. Donald Hayne. Englewood Cliffs, NJ: Prentice-Hall, 1959.
Finke, Laurie A. and Martin B. Shichtman. *Cinematic Illuminations: The Middle Ages on Film*. Baltimore, MD: John Hopkins University Press, 2010.
Forshey, Gerald E. *American Religious and Biblical Spectaculars*. Westport, CT: Praeger, 1992.
Gilchrist, Marianne McLeod. 'Bleedthrough: The Two-Way Traffic between Popular Historiography and Fiction'. *Journal of Historical Fictions* 2:1 (April 2019), pp. 18–44.
———. 'Getting away with Murder: Runciman and Conrad of Montferrat's Career in Constantinople'. *The Mediæval Journal* 2:1 (2012), pp. 15–36.
Hamilton, Bernard. *The Leper King and His Heirs*. Cambridge: CUP, 2000.
Irwin, Robert. 'Saladin and the Third Crusade: A Case Study in Historiography and the Historical Novel'. In *A Companion to Historiography*. ed. Michael Bentley. London: Routledge, 1997, pp. 139–52.
Kozlovic, Anton Karl. 'The Deep Focus Typecasting of Joseph Schildkraut as Judas Figure in Four DeMille Films'. *Journal of Religion and Popular Culture* 6 (Spring 2004). https://dspace.flinders.edu.au/xmlui/handle/2328/14270. [Accessed 29 September 2019].
Lamb, Harold. *The Flame of Islam*. New York: Doubleday, Doran & Co., 1930.
MacLeod, Anne Scott. 'Writing Backward: Modern Models in Historical Fiction'. *The Horn Book* (January–February 1998). www.hbook.com/1998/01/creating-books/publishing/writing-backward-modern-models-in-historical-fiction. [Accessed 20 September 2019].
Mills, Charles. *The History of Chivalry, or, Knighthood and its Times*. 3rd ed. London: Longman, Hurst, Rees, Orme, Brown and Green, 1825.
———. *The History of the Crusades for the Recovery and Possession of the Holy Land*. 3rd ed. London: Longman, Hurst, Rees, Orme and Brown, 1822.

Mitchell, Jerome. *Scott, Chaucer, and Medieval Romance: A Study in Sir Walter Scott's Indebtedness to the Literature of the Middle Ages.* Lexington, KY: University Press of Kentucky, 1987.

———. *The Walter Scott Operas: An Analysis of Operas Based on the Works of Sir Walter Scott.* Tuscaloosa, AL: University of Alabama Press, 1977.

Richards, Jeffrey. 'Sir Ridley Scott and the Rebirth of the Historical Epic'. In *The Return of the Epic Film: Genre, Aesthetics and History in the 21st Century.* ed. Andrew B.R. Elliott. Edinburgh: Edinburgh University Press, 2013, pp. 19–35.

Runciman, Steven. *A History of the Crusades.* 3 vols. Cambridge: CUP, 1951–4.

Siberry, Elizabeth. *The New Crusaders: Images of the Crusades in the Nineteenth and Early Twentieth Centuries.* Aldershot: Ashgate, 2000.

Tyerman, Christopher. *The Debate on the Crusades.* Manchester: MUP, 2011.

Vahimagi, Tise. 'Richard the Lionheart (1961–65)'. In *BFI: Screenonline.* London: British Film Institute, 2003–14. www.screenonline.org.uk/tv/id/1136160/synopsis.html. [Accessed 25 September 2019].

Whitaker, David. 'Doctor Who Photonovels: The Crusade'. *BBC Website.* London: BBC. www.bbc.co.uk/doctorwho/classic/photonovels/crusade. [Accessed 8 September 2019].

White, Henry Adelbert. *Sir Walter Scott's Novels on the Stage: A Dissertation.* New Haven CT: Yale University Press, 1927.

Wilcoxon, Henry and Katherine Orrison. *Lionheart in Hollywood: The Autobiography of Henry Wilcoxon.* Metuchen, NJ : Scarecrow Press, 1991.

5 Saladin and Richard the Lionheart
Entangled memories

Mike Horswell

In a dream sequence in Kamran Pasha's novel, *Shadow of the Swords* (2010), a feverish Richard the Lionheart sees a vision of the smoking ruins of a Jerusalem he has successfully conquered. Walking over the indistinguishable bodies of dead and dying combatants, Richard initially savours his victory: 'Jerusalem was his! The name of Richard the Lionheart would be inscribed in history alongside Alexander of Macedon, Julius Caesar, and Charles Martel.' In the dream, however, Richard's triumph is undercut. The English king encounters the crucifixion of Christ who, from the cross, challenges the integrity of Richard's crusading endeavour. Richard protests that he is dying for Christ, but the dream dramatically inverts his assertion:

> 'No, my son,' Christ said in a soft voice. 'It is I who die for you.' The figure raised his head, and Richard saw his blood-soaked bearded face. A sudden cold terror gripped Richard's heart. This was not his Lord, Jesus of Nazareth. [...] *The figure on the Cross was Saladin.*[1]

The mythologised encounters of King Richard I of England, known as 'the Lionheart', and Salah al-Din ibn Ayyub, the Kurdish Muslim leader known to the West as Saladin, are rarely so unexpected, or potent, as in the preceding example, but have proved a supple memory and source of inspiration ever since the two led opposing forces on the Third Crusade (1189–92). The reputations of Richard and Saladin individually transcend the Third Crusade and have taken on the trappings of heroism and villainy over the subsequent centuries. Although there is no record of them ever having met in person, this chapter explores manufactured memories of Richard and Saladin's meetings.

Jeffrey J. Cohen's *Medieval Identity Machines* considers how identities are constructed beyond the individual by examining the image of a knight on horseback.[2] In the composite assemblage of knight, armour, horse, and lance, the result is an identity which is more than the sum of its constituent parts; the 'knight-on-horseback' is an icon for a set of chivalric meanings, which can in turn be deployed for literary effect. Taking this prompt as a way to conceptualise identity beyond its individual embodiment, we can ask how a paired identity – a symbolic construction which exists only with the conjunction of multiple entities – might function in the case of Saladin and Richard.

This line of inquiry has already been taken up by Louise D'Arcens, Christine Chism, and John Ganim in their evaluation of Richard and Saladin's relationship(s) in film and literature. D'Arcens has argued that Saladin 'is generally placed into a homologous dyad with Richard I based on their mutual recognition and admiration for one another'.[3] They have been portrayed, Chism has suggested, 'Sometimes as ideal war-leaders bound by their honour and respect for each other and sometimes as inimical mutual nemeses [...] as the ultimate intimate enemies, or what we might today call "frenemies".'[4] Of their portrayal in Youssef Chahine's *El Naser Salah Ad-Din* (1963), Ganim wrote:

> the 'hero' of the film is not so much Saladin as it is a 'character' that is developed through the interaction of Saladin and Richard the Lionheart, and dramatic conflict is developed as much through Saladin's 'directing' of Richard, who becomes Saladin's double. Saladin is necessary for the full development of Richard's heroism, the film seems to say, just as Richard's own pride and the disunity and treachery of his forces serve as an admonitory lesson to the Arabs themselves.[5]

This chapter will complement the others in this volume by considering the meanings offered by the composite Richard-and-Saladin and their paired memory, rather than the memories and reputation of each leader individually.[6] Though authors of biographies of each leader have inevitably considered the other, the suggestion here is that drawing attention to the uniquely fused entity that is Richard-and-Saladin will allow focus on the ways in which identities – both that of a hero and a villain – are produced in and through, and reconfigured by, these assemblages.

Richard, Saladin, and the Third Crusade

Despite involving a host of European and Levantine aristocracy, the memory of the Third Crusade is dominated by the figures of Richard and Saladin. The death of Holy Roman Emperor Frederick Barbarossa on route to the Holy Land in 1190 and the return home of King Philip II of France after the siege of Acre in 1191 left the leadership of the crusade in Richard's hands, while no other Islamic figure in the region could challenge Saladin, conqueror of Jerusalem in 1187, who was at the peak of his power on the arrival of the crusaders. In addition to this pre-eminence, both Saladin and Richard repeatedly proved themselves masterful propagandists. Two contemporary biographers of Saladin – Baha' al-Din Ibn Shaddad and Imad al-Din al-Isfahani – were members of his inner circle, while 'in his own lifetime [Richard] became a deeply controversial figure at the centre of a violent propaganda war'.[7] Recognising this, the English king cultivated his reputation: he took a sword named after the legendary sword of King Arthur, Excalibur, on crusade.[8]

As events brought Richard and Saladin into closer proximity, the relationship between the adversaries was conducted through a combination of delicate diplomatic manoeuvres and continuing military abrasion. Ultimately, the crusade came to a negotiated end without the two ever meeting; Richard returned to Europe (via a period of captivity) and reigned until his death in 1199, while Saladin died in 1193. Chism has argued that in Western medieval literature Richard's memory has been deployed to symbolise division, Saladin's 'cultural entanglement'. Invoking Richard 'enacts implacable cultural conflict between Latin Christians and non-Latin Christians [...] Saladin stories thematise relationships across enemy lines, beneficial mutual alliance, and economies of breath-taking generosity'.[9]

Richard's memory over the centuries has fluctuated: from inclusion in a (Western) pantheon of heroes of the history of the world and possessing a reputation for chivalrous heroism in the medieval period, his character and competence were questioned by Enlightenment luminaries such as David Hume and Edward Gibbon.[10] While Richard's legend in the West appears to have moved from hero to villain (and possibly back in modern reappraisal), Saladin's has traced the opposite trajectory. Where medieval propagandists initially presented Saladin as an expression of demonic threat to Western Christendom – a 'son of Satan' and one of the seven heads of the Beast of the Apocalypse – by the thirteenth century he had become the honourable and chivalric opponent who could be 'claimed' for the West in various ways.[11] In the East, Saladin remained the liberator of Jerusalem and provided a to-hand model leader for resisting Western aggression from the nineteenth century to the present.[12]

The Third Crusade itself has rarely lacked historians or lapsed as a source of artistic inspiration. Felix Hinz' work on historical novels has found that to 2014, of the 551 novels he identified in English, French, and German relating to the crusades, more than a quarter are primarily concerned with the Third Crusade or its leaders (Saladin, Richard I, Phillip II, or Frederick Barbarossa).[13] This popularity has seen the Third Crusade transposed into other genres of popular culture: it has provided the setting for art, films, and digital games across the past two centuries. If the historical ending of the crusade proved unsatisfactory to Western Christians – Jerusalem had not been recovered – many over the subsequent centuries stepped in to fill the breach and offer substitute successes, however tenuous or imaginary. Sophie Cottin's 1805 novel *Mathilde*, for example, had the Muslim hero and his followers convert to Christianity at the conclusion of the novel, while the British General Allenby's capture of Jerusalem in 1917 was heralded in some quarters as completing Richard's mission.[14]

'A war between civilizations to be decided by a duel?'[15]

The Third Crusade seemed to contemporaries a titanic struggle, which could be personified as a duel between its leaders: 'Indeed a series of dramatic episodes in the crusade came to be perceived and presented both in literature and in decorative art as a personal duel between two individuals, Richard and Saladin.'[16] Many histories of the Third Crusade have adopted this approach and have framed their work through a confrontation between the Muslim sultan and the Christian king.[17]

The distillation of themes and conflict into the clash of two men was most clearly expressed by the medieval tale, found in the romance *Richard Coer de Lyon*, which had the leaders meet in mythic single combat. Saladin gave Richard a horse the colt of his own mare, trained to kneel to take milk from its mother when the mare whinnied. An angel appeared to Richard, however, and told him of the scheme and so Richard was able to frustrate it by stopping up the horse's ears. The climax of the encounter between Richard and Saladin saw the Angevin king unhorse Saladin – who managed to escape – and the crusaders defeat the Muslim army.[18] This episode formed part of a strategy to re-narrate the crusade as a successful, national endeavour.[19] The mythical duel of the two leaders welded them together as a quickly identifiable symbol of epic, chivalrous combat. This Richard-and-Saladin is epitomised by its appearance on decorative tiles and wall hangings from the thirteenth century: King Henry III of England commissioned the scene in 1251 and the Luttrell Psalter (*c*. 1325–35) contains a marginal image considered by some to be Richard and Saladin jousting (Figure 5.1).[20]

The duelling Richard-and-Saladin has resonated into the modern era. The one-time Jesuit French historian Louis Maimbourg imagined the combat between the two leaders as a chivalric encounter which occurred in the middle of a general battle in his 1675 account. Richard and Saladin simultaneously recognised one another on the battlefield and sought a definitive, individual fight:

> knowing each other by those Marks which distinguished them from the rest, they both hit upon the same thought, and each of them believing

Saladin and Richard the Lionheart 79

Figure 5.1 Figures believed to be Richard and Saladin jousting, Luttrell Psalter, *British Library*, BL Add MS 42130, fol. 82, c. 1325–1335. Image from *Wikimedia Commons*.

he had found an Enemy worthy of himself, and whom with honour he might combat, both as a Souldier [*sic*] and a King, they both believed that the general Victory would depend upon their particular Encounter, and that he whom Fortune should declare her Favourite, would not fail of having the Glory of singly obtaining the Victory. So both of them, at the same time, charging his Arm with a strong Lance, they furiously ran one against the other, [...] and *Richard* was something disordered with the mighty Blow which he received, but he had managed his Lance with so much Adress [*sic*] and Force, that he overthrew both Horse and Man upon the Ground.[21]

In his 1751 *Histoire des croisades*, Voltaire mentioned the encounter in passing, suggesting that the glory Richard won in unhorsing Saladin was almost all he took from the campaign.[22]

Though Joseph François Michaud's history of the crusades kept the adversaries separate, his work was reissued in 1877 with illustrations by Gustave Doré.[23] The last image, located with Michaud's concluding remarks, was a dramatic picture of a mounted and armoured Richard in the midst of combat at the battle of Arsuf (Figure 5.2). Although the title of the French edition did not mention Saladin, the English edition of 1880 captioned the same image, 'Richard Cœur de Lion and Saladin at the Battle of Arsur', and moved the image to accompany the narrative of the battle.[24] This relabelling has allowed the image to become associated with the mythical duel of the two. Moreover, the composition of the image echoes two earlier paintings which do present the duel.

The French artist Philippe Jacques de Loutherbourg (1740–1812) painted *The Battle between Richard Cœur de Lion and Saladin in Palestine* towards

Figure 5.2 Gustave Doré, 'Richard Cœur De Lion A La Bataille D'Arsur' in Joseph François Michaud, *Histoire des Croisades,* vol. 1 (Paris, 1877), pp. 368–69. Image from *Wikimedia Commons.*

the end of his life, while Abraham Cooper (1787–1868) depicted the same scene in his *Richard I called Coeur de Lion at the Battle of Ascalon in the Act of Unhorsing Saladin* (*c.* 1828).[25] Both featured Richard and Saladin centrally, on horseback, and showed Richard poised to strike a blow above

Saladin, whose horse was discomforted. In Cooper's composition Richard wore a red cross on a white tabard and a crown.

We have some sense of the propagation of these images through their imitations and use as illustrations. Loutherbourg's painting was reproduced as an engraving in Thomas Gaspey's *History of England* (1853) and William Adams' *The Wars of the Cross* (1883), while Cooper's work featured as an illustration in an issue of the *Boy's Herald* in 1877 and *Cassell's Children's Book of Knowledge* (1922–4).[26] His central image was included as a design for cameo brooches in which it was distilled to its core elements (Figure 5.3). The image was composed of the two riders in Cooper's poses – Richard preparing to strike, Saladin with upraised shield – as well as the other elements of Cohen's chivalric assemblage (the two horses, armour, helmets, and stirrups) and a slain figure and trampled flag at the bottom. Here the duel, as rendered by Cooper, is reduced to an iconic form.[27]

To return to Cohen's suggestion that identity can be distributed over assemblages, especially the chivalric array of horse–rider–armour–spurs, these images illustrate the process of hero-making. Out of the confused,

Figure 5.3 Cameo brooch from *c.* 1850s featuring the combat of Richard and Saladin from Abraham Cooper's 1828 painting. Image from Giovanna Di Rosa, antiquecameos.net. Reproduced with permission.

82 *Mike Horswell*

jumble of pieces of soldiers, horses, weapons, and shields – some discarded, some almost forming discrete figures – the artists have created whole assemblages at the centre of the pieces. Emphasised by the light in Cooper piece, Richard is the most complete figure in both: his horse, armour, weapon, and body are the most easily identified and coherent. Yet without Saladin each image would be incomplete – together they form a 'circuit or assemblage, a network of meaning' achieved only by the conjunction of Richard-and-Saladin as exemplifying the chivalric, identity-forming duel which battle was presented to Victorian Britons as providing.[28]

Other depictions of Saladin and Richard engaged in a personal duel reinforce the association of the two. Their imagined encounter was featured in a spectacular production of *Richard and Saladin or The Crusaders of Jerusalem* at Astley's amphitheatre in London in May 1843, and was employed through the nineteenth century in publications aimed at boys.[29] It continued to find utility into the twentieth century; the March 1966 edition of *Treasure* magazine included a colourful depiction of Richard knocking Saladin and his horse down.[30] These images propagated and essentialised a version of Richard-and-Saladin as locked in chivalric combat, embodying the intractability of Christian–Muslim conflict.

The sword and the scimitar: equal but opposite?

While important, the memory of Saladin and Richard engaged in single combat discussed in the foregoing do not represent the range of meanings which could be contained by the Richard-and-Saladin conjunction. If the duelling image could convey the energetic collision of two polar-opposite forces, other arrangements communicate different aspects of their paired memories, and imagined more complex encounters. These in turn illustrate the potential for the production of identity through the entanglement of the two together – the 'cancelling out' or silencing of their individuality, the contrasting of each against the other, and the potential for more dynamic encounters.

Sir Walter Scott's depictions of Richard-and-Saladin in *The Talisman* (1825) exemplified a dynamic, mirrored creation in ways which went on to be hugely influential.[31] Scott's much-quoted introduction (added in 1832) set up an inversion in the reader's expectations of a simple Richard-as-hero/Saladin-as-villain binary opposition:

> the warlike character of Richard I., wild and generous, a pattern of chivalry, with all its extravagant virtues, and its no less absurd errors, was opposed to that of Saladin, in which the Christian and English monarch showed all the cruelty and violence of an Eastern sultan, and

Saladin, on the other hand, displayed the deep policy and prudence of a European sovereign, whist each contended which should excel the other in the knightly qualities of bravery and generosity. This singular contrast afforded, as the author conceived, materials for a work of fiction possessing peculiar interest.[32]

It also suggests that it was the Richard-and-Saladin dynamic which Scott had initially seen as being the core of the novel.[33]

Chivalrous brethren

Scott's depiction of Richard-and-Saladin set the tone for subsequent portrayals. He echoed Maimbourg in suggesting an equality between the two based on chivalry; when they met, differences – apart from visual ones – were almost entirely erased:

> There was no need of further introduction. The two heroic monarchs, for such they both were, threw themselves at once from horseback, and, the troops halting and the music suddenly ceasing, they advanced to meet each other in profound silence, as brethren and equals.[34]

The moment of silence and descriptive absence is telling – the characters recognised an equal in the other and introduction was therefore pointless. Similarly, Henry Stebbing's *History of Chivalry and the Crusades* (1830) pitched Richard-and-Saladin as the pinnacle of chivalrous heroism. Amidst the signing of the treaty which concluded the Third Crusade he commented: 'But Saladin and Richard […] only gave each other a mutual promise of fidelity, the interchange of their parole being deemed a sufficient gage for the truth of heroes so brave and chivalrous as the Prince of the Saracens and the King of England.'[35] Their bravery and chivalry elevated them together to a plane above their contemporaries.

David Butler's film *King Richard and the Crusaders* (1954) was a loose adaptation of *The Talisman*.[36] An orientalised camp and gaudy Saladin variously disguised himself to observe an older, avuncular Richard; but neither Richard nor Saladin seemed to grow in the film – they ended it almost exactly as they began. The story culminated with Richard and Saladin, side-by-side, rendered observers as the Scottish hero Kenneth fought and killed the villain Amaury, Grand Master of the 'Castellans', and claimed Richard's cousin Edith as his wife. Saladin – his parting lines shouted in Arabic across the valley – ultimately retreated back into his previous identity, and Richard finished the film cheerfully looking forward to the prospect of more fighting at home.

This nullification of difference through the elevation of Saladin and Richard to the status of chivalric paragons is exemplified by themed chess sets which field 'crusaders vs. Muslims' with Richard and Saladin as king-pieces; their movement and forces are exactly matched and differ only in appearance.[37]

Opposites

But this essential similarity did not always obliterate difference. Scott used their parity of stature to underscore the characters' deviations. In *The Talisman*, Richard's physical strength was contrasted with Saladin's sharpness in a much-repeated feat of arms of the author's invention, namely when Richard chopped through an iron mace with his sword, and in response Saladin sliced a silk cushion and then a veil with his scimitar.[38] This episode could be freighted according to taste. To some it was a celebration of difference: the popular Ladybird children's history of Richard in 1965 concluded: 'Each weapon was perfect in its own way.'[39] Paul Creswick's 1904 novel *With Richard the Fearless*, however, had Saladin surrender to the hero Peter when the Muslim leader's sword broke in battle against him. In a riposte to Scott's 'equal-but-different' motif, here English was best: 'The Saracen's light blade shivered and snapped against the English iron.' Peter then delivered Saladin to Richard, who magnanimously released him and so precipitated the peaceful conclusion of the crusade.[40] Equal-but-different is the approach taken by games such as *Kings' Crusade* (2010) and *Stronghold Crusader II* (2014) which feature the two as leaders of opposed factions each of which has different units, mechanics of play, strengths, and weaknesses, as well as aesthetics.

In *The Talisman*, Saladin is a model of restrained application of power while Richard is 'out of control, unaware of what is happening, and a much less efficient politician'. Indeed, Saladin's mastery of healing and justice, through talisman and scimitar respectively, granted him 'control of the plot itself; without him there would be no just conclusion'.[41] Richard's role in the novel reflected this – though in the foreground of the action, he was reactive to events around him. In contrast, and setting a trend which many would follow in subsequent centuries, Saladin appeared throughout in disguises which granted him agency in the plot. He was an emir, a physician, and as the Sultan he hosted the climactic duel between Kenneth and Conrade (Marquis of Montserrat and one of the novel's villains) and dispensed justice in killing the Templar Grand Master. Though this latter feat is an historic episode transplanted from Saladin's execution of Raynald of Châtillon after the Battle of Hattin, Richard's presence here amplified the contrast between his passivity and Saladin's decisiveness.

Moreover, the difference between the two which could not ultimately be overcome was their faith. The characters recognised Saladin's essential chivalric equality and attempted to reconcile it to their own political structures in the suggestion that he marry Richard's cousin Edith. Historically, the proposal to end the crusade through the marriage of Richard's sister Joan to Saladin's brother Saphadin (Sayf al-Din) and have them both rule from Jerusalem seems to have been speculative; here its rejection by Edith and Saladin reveals the insurmountable fracture faith presented to Saladin's full adoption by the Christian West.[42]

Celestia A. Bloss' *Heroines of the Crusades* (1853) liberally mixed history, legend, and imagined characters and events. She too sought resolution for the Third Crusade through chivalrous encounter between Richard and Saladin. Bloss had the leaders meet at the conclusion of the peace treaty negotiations where, like Stebbing's 1830 account mentioned earlier, 'distaining the common obligation of an oath' they shook hands over the treaty, their word being sufficient to guarantee its efficacy.[43] Saladin was granted agency in the vignette – it was he who arranged the treaty camp with the leaders' tents as the opposing poles, and he who sought Richard out for a conversation. Traversing the physical distance between the two, Saladin was also depicted as crossing the cultural divide: he spoke to Richard in his 'mother-tongue' to the latter's surprise, and confessed his adolescent love for Eleanor of Aquitaine, Richard's mother, whom he sought news of. Drawing on late medieval myths of Saladin's romantic involvement with Eleanor and other Western women, Bloss suggested that Saladin could be integrated into Western mythology, causing Richard to assume Saladin could be claimed for the West as a crypto-Christian – 'Thou art a Christian in thy secret heart' he exclaimed.[44] Saladin rebuffed him, again restoring the Christian–Muslim dichotomy as primary and irreducible. Bloss' imagined account exemplified the oppositions that Richard-and-Saladin could embody in the moment of meeting: Saladin's agency and Richard's passivity, Richard's impulsive jumping to conclusions against Saladin's decades-held secret, and the Muslim East and the Christian West.

Bloss' Richard-and-Saladin is a quintessential expression of civilizational encounter, wherein each leader embodied 'the character and the destiny of the nations which they represented'. Richard – younger and virile – emerged in a better light due to a teleological nineteenth-century perspective on the fortunes of races and nations:

> In the compact and muscular frame, and sparkling eyes of Richard, were expressed that reckless spirit of pursuit, that ardor of passion, enthusiasm, born of conscious strength and indomitable will, which

characterized the growing nations of Europe, and finally gave the dominion of the world to the Anglo-Saxon race.[45]

But it was the mutual recognition of Saladin and Richard's chivalry – their essential equality – which again here diffused the conflict of the Third Crusade and explained its conclusion.

'We will walk through the gates of Jerusalem together': potent encounters

Reflecting their historical separation direct encounters between Richard and Saladin are rarer than might be expected, especially in modern crusading literature. Stories of the Third Crusade often set the pair as poles whose lines of influence framed the boundaries of the field in which an intermediate hero could freely move, and subsequently encounter both leaders. This was case, for example, for George A. Henty's hero Cuthbert in his *Winning His Spurs* (1882) and in Ronald Welch's Carnegie Medal winning *Knight Crusader* (1954).[46] While films such as Ridley Scott's *Kingdom of Heaven* (2005) and those featuring Robin Hood made one of Richard or Saladin peripheral, others have centred the Richard-and-Saladin dynamic, 'a strategy inspired by the charismatic pairing of well-matched antagonists'.[47] These invocations of Saladin and Richard are more complex, allowing versions of Richard-and-Saladin which produce heroism and villainy in less reductive ways.

The Talisman influenced almost all crusading films of the twentieth century, and was directly adapted, and embellished, in films of 1911, 1923, 1954; a British television drama of 1980–1; and a Russian two-part film in 1992–3.[48] Cecille B. DeMille's Hollywood blockbuster *The Crusades* (1935) drew on Scott's novel – the trial of strength scene in which Richard cuts through an iron mace before Saladin slices a silk veil is repeated.[49] Unlike many other depictions of Richard-and-Saladin, 'both undergo dramatic transformations' which were, according to John Aberth, 'entirely unconvincing'.[50] The two were directly opposed through their conflict over the possession of Acre, Jerusalem, and Berengaria, Richard's Navarrese wife; the competition catalysed their transformations. Where Richard found faith and a love for his wife as he increasingly took the crusade seriously, Saladin flickered between the despotic persecutor of the Eastern Christians, a chivalrous suitor of Berengaria, and the magnanimous and honourable opponent of the crusaders.[51] 'By Allah, I wish you might have been my brother, not my foe', Saladin responded to Richard's impetuous individual invasion of his tent in pursuit of Berengaria. The two were framed squarely as equals, the mutual respect bringing about Saladin's terms for peace, including the return of Berengaria and the end of the crusade, but not before Richard refused the kingship of Jerusalem offered at the price of his conversion to Islam. Once again, difference was figured religiously, despite Richard's admission of his own lack of faith. Richard's pride – and sword – were broken by the terms which excluded the fulfilment of his own crusading vow, leaving him penitent and prayerful, and again without agency. It was left to Saladin to be the guarantor of the peace and dispenser of justice. The inconsistency of Saladin and 'conversion' of Richard in DeMille's film highlights their lack of change elsewhere – especially in Butler's 1954 production.

The 1963 Egyptian film *El Naser Salah el Dine*, directed by Youssef Chahine, celebrated Saladin as a magnanimous, religiously tolerant, anti-imperialist – a 'retribution' to Western crusading films.[52] Richard needed Saladin's help to foil plots in the crusader camp and once again Saladin in disguise healed Richard's wound. This *Talisman*-inspired trope reinforced the image of Saladin's mastery of healing and his freedom to move unmolested through hostile territory. In fact, this Richard-and-Saladin is one in which Saladin leads Richard from warmongering ignorance to enlightenment of the futility of his aggressive invasion of Arab lands. The English king 'realizes that his own people, rather than Saladin, are the enemies of Christian principles'.[53] Richard, come to make peace on Saladin's terms, admits that he could not tell the crusader and Arab corpses apart; Saladin thanks him for 'being the Richard I've always imagined'.[54] The film was consistent throughout with then Egyptian president Gamal Nasser's political aims which were embodied by Saladin: he was a pan-Arab nationalist, anti-imperialist, and anti-capitalist. In fact Saladin is overdetermined by this image: 'Saladin does not falter, does not fail, and will never die', leaving his character 'more of an icon than a man'. He has no narrative development, 'only a meteoric rise because of innate, unfaltering, superhuman virtue'.[55] Richard-and-Saladin here is, as Ganim has argued, a didactic dyad which served to reveal Saladin's qualities.

The play *Holy Warriors*, performed during the summer of 2014 at the London Globe theatre, explored the resonance of the encounter on the Third Crusade between Richard and Saladin. David Eldridge's 'fantasia' juxtaposed the medieval crusade with modern conflicts, drawing continuities between the First World War, Arab-Israeli wars, and the Iraq Wars. Richard appeared emblazoned with his iconic gold lions on a red background and later dressed in modern desert combat fatigues: the crusaders 'look like serving soldiers in Iraq' read one scripted instruction.[56] The play imagined a counterfactual possibility for enduring peace through its meeting of Richard and Saladin. After the conclusion of their crusade-ending treaty, Saladin offered Richard the opportunity to visit Jerusalem as a pilgrim (echoing Chahine's film), stating: 'I will welcome you myself. We will walk through the gates of Jerusalem together and such a deed will be remembered for all of time' – an offer to defuse the animosity and violence embodied by the crusade.[57] The English king, however, refused to complete his pilgrimage to the Holy City in peace. Instead, the final scene connected his devotion to holy war with violence in the Middle East, the 9/11 terror attacks by Al-Qaeda in the United States, and the subsequent 'War on Terror'. Eldridge imagined Saladin presenting Richard the Lionheart with an opportunity to repent and to turn the Third Crusade into a symbol of reconciliation; instead, he chose perpetual civilizational strife. The play ended with the arrival of George W. Bush, US president in 2001, who threw Richard a sword as he repeated his famous invocation of the crusades which inaugurated the 'War on Terror': 'This crusade. This war on terrorism. Its gonna take a while.'[58]

Perhaps most provocative is the example this chapter opened with. In Pasha's novel, written in response to 9/11, Richard's vision of the crucified Christ wore the visage of Saladin, while the centurion who speared Christ's side bore Richard's own face. The dream-ridden novel presented Richard and Saladin as enmeshed in a love triangle with the Jewish Miriam, which provided a domestic tension around which the fate of the crusade revolved. The novel concluded with a swordfight between the two 'archenemies'. While Richard was prevented from killing Saladin by a vivid recollection of his earlier vision, Saladin in turn refused to kill Richard, pronouncing that it was not 'fitting for kings to tear each other apart like rabid dogs', and the two settled a truce between them.[59]

Many depictions of Richard-and-Saladin, then, have allowed for more complex interactions than the duel motif, or even a stultifying equivalence. The presentations of Saladin and Richard are often mutually constitutive, especially of their fraternal chivalric respect. One may eclipse the other – as in Chahine's film – and their proximity can be employed to highlight their differences for various ends. In Eldridge's play and Pasha's novel we see both given the opportunity to develop and exercise agency over the course of the events which brought them together. Finally, their conjunction can offer fascinating counterfactual suggestions or potent new configurations for thinking about their relation to one another, the Third Crusade, and the history of religious violence.

Conclusion

In the conjunction of Richard-and-Saladin we see the potential for thinking about heroes and villains differently. Rather than considering the reputation of each individually and tracing its fluctuations, this perspective allows us to consider how identity is collectively constructed and maintained. It allows us to consider the memory of historical figures as the product of intersecting actions and reputations, foregrounding the ways in which collective memories are entangled. Moving helpfully away from binary oppositions of hero/villain, Richard-and-Saladin asks new questions of how each is remembered in the light of the other and how they construct one another. Occasionally the conjunction produces creative, innovative encounters – either positioning the two dynamically in tension, highlighting their differences, or having them annihilate each other's distinctiveness in their bland monotony of elevated chivalry. Pasha's Saladin-as-Christ stands out as an extraordinary attempt to reframe the relationship between antagonists and religions, but often the effort to have the encounter be meaningful in civilisational or philosophical terms leaves the leaders overwritten by the larger narrative imperatives of the creator. Chahine's Saladin-as-paragon needs Richard as a slow-learning pupil, revealing in turn the glory of Saladin/ Nasser, while Bloss' imagined encounter illustrates a supposed moment of racial comparison and glimpse at historical destiny.

Richard-and-Saladin is a product of frustrated (usually Western) desire: a desire for a titanic, definitive clash which would 'settle once and for all who was the greatest'; a desire for a less complicated, ambiguous end to the Third Crusade; and a desire to know what would happen if these two paragons of chivalry had ever met in person. Like two stars drawn into each other's paths, the reputations of Richard and Saladin have orbited one another, perpetually locked together in orbit like a binary star. This paired set of forces interact, creating a single, dynamic entity from two held together: the memory of Richard-and-Saladin.

Notes

1 Kamran Pasha, *Shadow of the Swords* (London, 2010), p. 189.
2 Jeffrey J. Cohen, *Medieval Identity Machines* (London, 2001).
3 Louise D'Arcens, 'The Crusades and Medievalism' in *The Cambridge Companion to the Literature of the Crusades*, ed. Anthony Bale (Cambridge, 2019), p. 254.
4 Christine Chism, 'Saladin and Richard I' in Bale, ed., *Literature of the Crusades*, p. 169.
5 John M. Ganim, 'Reversing the Crusades: Hegemony, Orientalism, and Film Language in Youssef Chahine's Saladin' in *Race, Class, and Gender in 'Medieval' Cinema*, eds. Lynn T. Ramey and Tison Pugh (New York, 2007), p. 54.
6 See John Gillingham, *Richard I* (London, 2002); J.L. Nelson, ed., *Richard Coeur De Lion in History and Myth* (London, 1992); Chism, 'Saladin and Richard I'; Phillips, *Saladin*.
7 Gillingham, *Richard I*, p. 4.
8 Ibid., p. 3; Thomas Asbridge, *Richard I* (London, 2019), pp. 95–6.
9 Chism, 'Saladin and Richard I', p. 171.
10 Gillingham, *Richard I*, pp. 1–2.
11 Phillips, *Saladin*, pp. 315–28.
12 Ibid., pp. 329–86.

13 That is 147; of which 82 (of a total of 274) are in English, 51 (of 207) are in German, and 14 (of 70) are in French; Felix Hinz, ed., *Kreuzzüge des Mittelalters und der Neuzeit* (Hildesheim, 2015), pp. 335–63.
14 Megan L. Morris, 'Madame Cottin's The Saracen, or Matilda and Malek Adhel', *The Crusades Project,* University of Rochester, <https://web.archive.org/web/20200131160848/https://d.lib.rochester.edu/crusades/text/saracen-or-matlda>, [accessed 31 January 2020]; Mike Horswell, *The Rise and Fall of British Crusader Medievalism, c. 1825–1945* (Abingdon, 2018), pp. 124–31.
15 Pasha, *Shadow*, p. 372.
16 Gillingham, *Richard I*, p. 3.
17 E.g. Geoffrey Regan, *Lionhearts: Saladin and Richard I* (London, 1998); James Reston, *Warriors of God: Richard the Lionheart and Saladin in the Third Crusade* (London, 2001).
18 Roger Sherman Loomis, 'Richard Cœur de Lion and the Pas Saladin in Medieval Art', *PMLA* 30:3 (1915), pp. 512–13; John Gillingham, 'Some Legends of Richard the Lionheart: Their Development and Their Influence' in Nelson, ed., *Richard*, pp. 53–4.
19 Geraldine Heng, *Empire of Magic* (New York, 2003), pp. 77–8.
20 Loomis, 'Medieval Art', pp. 513–18; Gillingham, 'Legends of Richard', p. 54; Chism, 'Saladin and Richard I', pp. 167–9; The Luttrell Psalter, *British Library*, p. 10, <https://www.bl.uk/onlinegallery/ttp/luttrell/accessible/pages9and10.html>, [accessed 12 November 2019].
21 Louis Maimbourg, *The History of the Crusade*, trans. John Nalson (London, 1685), p. 207.
22 'Richard eut la gloire de désarçonner Saladin; ce fut presque tout ce qu'il gagna dans cette expédition mémorable.' Voltaire, *Histoire des croisades* (1751), pp. 62–3.
23 Joseph François Michaud, *Histoire des croisades*, vol. 1 (Paris, 1877), pp. 368–9.
24 Joseph François Michaud, *History of the Crusades*, trans. W. Robson (Philadelphia, 1880), pp. 262–3. This misattribution has been copied by later distributors of Doré's images.
25 Siberry, *New Crusaders*, p. 163.
26 Thomas Gaspey, *The History of England*, vol. 1 (London, 1853), pp. 206–7; William H.D. Adams, *The Wars of the Cross, or The History of the Crusades* (London, 1883), pp. 90, 93; *Boy's Herald*, 17 November 1877, vol. 2, p. 319; Harold F.B. Wheeler, ed., *Cassell's Children's Book of Knowledge*, 8 vols. (London, 1922).
27 See Giovanna Di Rosa, 'Cameo of King Richard I', *Antique Cameos, c.* 1850s, <https://web.archive.org/web/20191112165348/https://antiquecameos.net/cameos/cameo-of-king-richard-i-6298215388>, [accessed 14 November 2019].
28 Cohen, *Medieval Identity Machines*, p. 76; Mark Girouard, *Return to Camelot* (London, 1981).
29 Siberry, *New Crusaders*, p. 147; 'The Combat Between Richard and Saladin', *Illustrated London News*, 20 May 1843, p. 343; e.g. 'Tales of Chivalry', *Boy's Herald*, 19 May 1877, p. 317.
30 Peter Jackson, 'When They Were Young: Richard the Lion Heart', *Treasure* 167 (26 March 1966).
31 Siberry, *New Crusaders*, pp. 112–30.
32 Walter Scott, *The Talisman*, vol. 38, The Waverley Novels (Edinburgh, 1860), p. 5.

33 There is a strong argument that the finished novel depends more on the triad of Richard-Saladin-Kenneth; Alice Chandler, 'Chivalry and Romance: Scott's Medieval Novels', *Studies in Romanticism* 14:2 (1975), p. 198.
34 Scott, *The Talisman*, pp. 492–3.
35 Henry Stebbing, *The History of Chivalry and the Crusades*, vol. 2 (Edinburgh, 1830), p. 142.
36 David Butler, *King Richard and the Crusaders* (Hollywood, CA, 1954).
37 E.g. *Lionheart Designs*, <http://lionheart-designs.com/yeOldeCountyFaire/Chess/Europe/Richard%20vs%20Saladin%20Crusades.shtml>; *Chess House*, <https://web.archive.org/web/20200213165236/https://www.chesshouse.com/products/richard-the-lionheart-chess-set>, both [accessed 13 February 2020].
38 Scott, *The Talisman*, pp. 495–8.
39 Lawrence Du Garde Peach, *Richard the Lion Heart* (Loughborough, 1965), p. 26.
40 Paul Creswick, *With Richard the Fearless* (London, 1904), p. 235.
41 David Simpson, '"Which Is the Merchant Here? And Which the Jew?": Friends and Enemies in Walter Scott's Crusader Novels', *Studies in Romanticism* 47:4 (2008), p. 443.
42 Phillips, *Saladin*, p. 269; Scott, *The Talisman*, pp. 478–80.
43 Celestia A. Bloss, *Heroines of the Crusades* (Muscatine, IA, 1853), p. 262.
44 Phillips, *Saladin*, p. 321; Bloss, *Heroines*, p. 260.
45 Ibid., p. 262.
46 George A. Henty, *Winning His Spurs* (London, 1882); Ronald Welch, *Knight Crusader* (Oxford, 1954).
47 Lorraine Kochanske Stock, 'Now Starring in the Third Crusade: Depictions of Richard I and Saladin in Films and Television Series' in *Hollywood in the Holy Land*, p. 98.
48 See Hervé Dumont, *Encyclopédie du film historique*, <www.hervedumont.ch>, [accessed 8 November 2019].
49 Cecille B. DeMille, *The Crusades* (Hollywood, CA, 1935).
50 John Aberth, *A Knight at the Movies* (London, 2003), p. 88.
51 Ibid., pp. 87–9.
52 Youssef Chahine, *El Naser Salah el Dine* (Cairo, 1963); Paul B. Sturtevant, 'SaladiNasser: Nasser's Political Crusade in El Naser Salah Ad-Din' in *Hollywood in the Holy Land*, p. 142.
53 Ganim, 'Reversing the Crusades', p. 53.
54 Aberth, *Knight at the Movies*, p. 103.
55 Sturtevant, 'SaladiNasser', pp. 128–30.
56 David Eldridge, *Holy Warriors* (London, 2014), p. 62.
57 Ibid., p. 92.
58 Ibid., p. 94.
59 Pasha, *Shadow*, pp. 190, 373.

Bibliography

Primary

Adams, William H.D. *The Wars of the Cross, or The History of the Crusades*. London: T. Nelson and Sons, 1883.

Bloss, Celestia A. *Heroines of the Crusades*. Muscatine, IA: R.M. Burnett, 1853.
Butler, David. *King Richard and the Crusaders*. Hollywood, CA: Warner Bros., 1954.
Chahine, Youssef. *El Naser Salah el Dine*. Cairo: Lotus Films, 1963.
Creswick, Paul. *With Richard the Fearless: A Tale of the Red Crusade*. London: E. Nister, 1904.
DeMille, Cecille B. *The Crusades*. Hollywood, CA: Universal Pictures, 1935.
Di Rosa, Giovanna. 'Cameo of King Richard I'. *Antique Cameos*. web.archive.org/web/20191112165348/https://antiquecameos.net/cameos/cameo-of-king-richard-i-6298215388. [Accessed 14 November 2019].
Du Garde Peach, Lawrence. *Richard the Lion Heart*. Ladybird History 561. Loughborough: Wills & Hepworth, 1965.
Eldridge, David. *Holy Warriors*. London: Bloomsbury, 2014.
Gaspey, Thomas. *The History of England*. 8 vols. London: London Printing and Publishing, 1853.
Henty, George A. *Winning His Spurs*. London: Sampson Low, Marston, Searle, & Rivington, 1882.
Jackson, Peter. 'When They Were Young: Richard the Lion Heart'. *Treasure* 167 (26 March 1966). https://web.archive.org/save/https://www.lookandlearn.com/history-images/A001043/Richard-I-the-Lion-Heart?t=2&q=Peter+Jackson&n=14. [Accessed 24 April 2020].
Maimbourg, Louis. *The History of the Crusade; or the Expeditions of the Christian Princes for the Conquest of the Holy Land*. Trans. John Nalson. London: R.H., 1685.
Michaud, Joseph François. *Histoire des croisades*. 3 vols. Paris: L'Academie Française, 1877.
———. *History of the Crusades*. Trans. W. Robson. 2 vols. Philadelphia, PA: George Barrie, 1880.
Pasha, Kamran. *Shadow of the Swords: An Epic Novel of the Crusades*. London: Washington Square Press, 2010.
Scott, Walter. *The Talisman*. Edinburgh: Adam and Charles Black, 1860.
Stebbing, Henry. *The History of Chivalry and the Crusades*. 2 vols. Edinburgh: Constable, 1830.
'Tales of Chivalry'. *Boy's Herald*, 19 May 1877, p. 317.
'The Combat between Richard and Saladin'. *Illustrated London News*, 20 May 1843, p. 343.
The Luttrell Psalter. *British Library*. www.bl.uk/onlinegallery/ttp/luttrell/accessible/pages9and10.html. [Accessed 12 November 2019].
Voltaire. *Histoire des croisades*. A. Berlin, 1751.
Welch, Ronald. *Knight Crusader*. Oxford: OUP, 1954.
Wheeler, Harold F.B., ed. *Cassell's Children's Book of Knowledge*. 8 vols. London: Waverly Book Co., 1922–24.

Secondary

Aberth, John. *A Knight at the Movies: Medieval History on Film*. London: Routledge, 2003.
Asbridge, Thomas. *Richard I*. London: Penguin, 2019.

Chandler, Alice. 'Chivalry and Romance: Scott's Medieval Novels'. *Studies in Romanticism* 14 (1975), pp. 185–200.

Chism, Christine. 'Saladin and Richard I'. In *The Cambridge Companion to the Literature of the Crusades.* ed. Anthony Bale. Cambridge: CUP, 2019, pp. 167–83.

Cohen, Jeffrey J. *Medieval Identity Machines.* London: University of Minnesota Press, 2001.

D'Arcens, Louise. 'The Crusades and Medievalism'. In *The Cambridge Companion to the Literature of the Crusades.* ed. Anthony Bale. Cambridge: CUP, 2019, pp. 248–62.

Dumont, Hervé. *Encyclopédie du film historique.* www.hervedumont.ch. [Accessed 8 November 2019].

Ganim, John M. 'Reversing the Crusades: Hegemony, Orientalism, and Film Language in Youssef Chahine's Saladin'. In *Race, Class, and Gender in 'Medieval' Cinema.* eds. Lynn T. Ramey and Tison Pugh. New York: Palgrave Macmillan, 2007, pp. 45–58.

Gillingham, John. *Richard I.* London: Yale University Press, 2002.

──────. 'Some Legends of Richard the Lionheart. Their Development and Their Influence'. In *Richard Coeur De Lion in History and Myth.* ed. J.L. Nelson. London: King's College London Centre for Medieval Studies, 1992, pp. 51–69.

Girouard, Mark. *Return to Camelot.* London: Yale University Press, 1981.

Heng, Geraldine. *Empire of Magic: Medieval Romance and the Politics of Cultural Fantasy.* New York: Columbia University Press, 2003.

Hinz, Felix, ed. *Kreuzzüge des Mittelalters und der Neuzeit.* Hildesheim: Georg Olms Verlag, 2015.

Horswell, Mike. *The Rise and Fall of British Crusader Medievalism, c. 1825–1945.* Abingdon: Routledge, 2018.

Loomis, Roger Sherman. 'Richard Cœur de Lion and the Pas Saladin in Medieval Art'. *PMLA* 30 (1915), pp. 509–28.

Morris, Megan L. 'Madame Cottin's The Saracen, or Matilda and Malek Adhel'. *The Crusades Project, University of Rochester.* https://web.archive.org/web/20200131160848/https://d.lib.rochester.edu/crusades/text/saracen-or-matlda. [Accessed 31 January 2020].

Phillips, Jonathan. *The Life and Legend of the Sultan Saladin.* London: Bodley Head, 2019.

Regan, Geoffrey. *Lionhearts: Saladin and Richard I.* London: Constable, 1998.

Reston, James. *Warriors of God: Richard the Lionheart and Saladin in the Third Crusade.* London: Doubleday, 2001.

Siberry, Elizabeth. *The New Crusaders: Images of the Crusades in the 19th and Early 20th Centuries.* Aldershot: Ashgate, 2000.

Simpson, David. '"Which Is the Merchant Here? And Which the Jew?": Friends and Enemies in Walter Scott's Crusader Novels'. *Studies in Romanticism* 47 (2008), pp. 437–52.

Stock, Lorraine Kochanske. 'Now Starring in the Third Crusade: Depictions of Richard I and Saladin in Films and Television Series'. In *Hollywood in the*

Holy Land: Essays on Film Depictions of the Crusades and Christian-Muslim Clashes, eds. Nickolas Haydock and Edward L. Risden. London: McFarland & Company, 2009, pp. 97–122.

Sturtevant, Paul B. 'SaladiNasser: Nasser's Political Crusade in El Naser Salah Ad-Din'. In *Hollywood in the Holy Land: Essays on Film Depictions of the Crusades and Christian-Muslim Clashes*. eds. Nickolas Haydock and Edward L. Risden. London: McFarland & Company, 2009, pp. 123–46.

6 Saint Louis
A crusader king and hero for Victorian and First World War Britain and Ireland

Elizabeth Siberry

King Louis IX of France, who was canonised as Saint Louis in 1297, has been remembered by his fellow countrymen as an exemplary Christian ruler; anniversaries of his birth in 1214 and death in 1270 continue to be marked by celebratory publications, events, and exhibitions. He was known for his personal devotion, and this was reflected in his commissioning of the Sainte Chapelle in Paris. A masterpiece of Gothic architecture, it was built to house relics of the Passion, including Christ's Crown of Thorns, purchased from Baldwin II, the Latin emperor of Constantinople. Louis led two crusades, although neither achieved their military goals. The first ended with the disastrous defeat at Mansurah in Egypt in 1250 and Louis's own captivity, but he then made his way to the Holy Land and stayed in the Latin Kingdom until 1254, playing a key role in rebuilding and refortifying its defences. His second crusade ended with his death from disease outside the walls of Tunis.

There have been detailed studies of how Saint Louis has been remembered in nineteenth-century France,[1] but this chapter will consider how he came to be regarded – perhaps surprisingly – as an important Christian exemplar and hero in nineteenth- and early twentieth-century Britain and Ireland. This period was rich in examples of works inspired by the crusades and Saint Louis, particularly as described by his biographer Jean de Joinville, became the subject of numerous biographies, poems, and novels, by a wide range of authors. He was also depicted in a number of stained-glass windows throughout the British Isles, as a saintly hero and warrior, to commemorate those who had fallen in later conflicts and especially the First World War, much of which of course was fought on French soil.

Reading and reviewing history

As the nineteenth century progressed, those interested in the history of France and the crusading movement had a selection of works to read, and

96 *Elizabeth Siberry*

these were quite widely available in the growing number of public lending libraries as well as private collections. There were general histories of Europe in the Middle Ages such as Henry Hallam's popular *View of the State of Europe During the Middle Ages* (published in 1818 and running to numerous editions thereafter) and works specifically devoted to the crusades.[2] For example, Charles Mills' *History of the Crusades* was published in 1820, and in 1852 William Robson published his English translation of Joseph François Michaud's history, although many seem to have been already familiar with it in the original French (*Histoire des croisades*, 1811–22).[3]

Joinville's *Histoire de Saint Louis* was also widely available, in a variety of editions and translations. In 1807, Cardiganshire landowner Thomas Johnes published his own translation of Joinville using his private Hafod Press, and copies of his translation could (and still can) be found in country house libraries.[4] These books were not just to impress visitors or for decorative purposes with fine leather bindings. They were used and read, and some country house libraries served as a form of local lending library for friends, neighbours, and staff.[5] As an example, the popular novelist and author of history textbooks Charlotte Yonge wrote a novel in 1866 about Prince Edward of England's crusade (1271–2), *The Prince and the Page*,[6] and made use of the libraries at Hursley Park, near her home in Hampshire and at Tyntesfield in Somerset (the home of her friends the Gibbs family), as well as the collection of Winchester College school. These allowed her, in the words of one biographer, to 'read printed sources and keep abreast of new research'.[7] This was also the era when major town and city libraries were being established, and published catalogues show that editions and translations of Joinville could be found in public libraries in, for example, Birmingham, Edinburgh, Glasgow, Manchester, Newcastle, and Norwich.

Books (in English and other European languages) were advertised and reviewed in the plethora of periodicals that appeared during the nineteenth century, and these reached an audience much wider than their individual subscriber base. Such reviews could also run to more than 10 pages and discussed not only the work itself but also the merits of the crusades as a whole. For example, an anonymous reviewer in the *Edinburgh Review* of 1809 did not consider Joinville a talented author but read the *Memoirs* 'with exceeding pleasure, from their interesting subject'. He also seems to have been familiar with the manuscript and publishing history of the work and discussed in some critical detail the way in which Thomas Johnes had approached his subject:

> The public should know that the real Joinville differs from that which Mr Johnes has translated not only in every page but almost in every

sentence [...] Perhaps we may be thought to bear hard upon a gentleman whose preference of literary recreations to those more usual among his class does him unquestionable honour [...] but whatever respect is due to a country squire who translates French chroniclers, we cannot at once give him a high place in the republic of letters.[8]

The *Critical Review* similarly noted some 'defects of inattention' but the reviewer of the *Monthly Review or Literary Journal* was more enthusiastic:

> We congratulate our countrymen on the opportunity they now have of becoming acquainted with the shrewd and ingenious Lord of Joinville, and with the pious St. Louis, his friend and master, one of the best kings with whom any age has been blessed.[9]

But whatever its imperfections, the first edition soon sold out and a plan to meet the public demand with a supplementary volume was prevented only by the disastrous fire at Hafod in 1807.[10]

In his 1840 catalogue of books for sale, the London bookseller James Bohn had two copies of Johnes on offer.[11] His publisher brother Henry reprinted Johnes' translation in a more affordable edition, as part of *Bohn's Standard Library*. The prospectus advertised it as:

> A series of the best English and Foreign authors, printed in a new and elegant form, equally adapted to the library and the fireside at the extremely low price of 3s 6d per volume [...] [a] series [...] undertaken with the view of presenting to the educated public works of a deservedly established character, accurately printed [...] without abridgement.

Bohn's *Joinville* seems to have been popular, with several editions in the second half of the nineteenth century and was again purchased by a number of public libraries.

In 1868, James Hutton published another translation of Joinville, this time in the Bayard series of 'choice books for home and abroad comprising history, biography, travel, essays (and) novelettes' at a price of half a crown. The publishers (Sampson, Low and Marston in Ludgate Hill, London) stated that their aim was:

> To put forward good books, pure and sound in morals [...] to produce them in such an elegant and recherche style as to make them really attractive to all classes of readers; and they wish especially to add that each work may be relied upon as having undergone careful editing, and being complete in itself.[12]

The new translation was advertised as real history which, quoting from a review in the *Times*:

> Widens our minds and our hearts and gives us that true knowledge of the world and of human nature in all its phases which but few men can gain in the short span of their own life and in the narrow sphere of their friends and enemies. We can hardly imagine a better book for boys to read and men to ponder over. [13]

Hutton's translation ran through numerous editions (15 between 1868 and 1910) and it must have been widely available in public and circulating libraries, as well as private collections. It may also have been available in school libraries – my own copy has a bookplate from Malvern College. Authors also seem to have drawn on Joinville for stories that would interest and benefit their young readers, with an abridged version entitled *Stories of Olden Times* published in 1870.[14]

The life of Saint Louis, as described by Joinville, remained attractive to translators and publishers throughout this period, and in 1906, Ethel Wedgwood, wife of the first Lord Wedgwood (great-great grandson of the potter Josiah Wedgwood) and herself a political activist and reformer, published a new English version of Joinville, which she declared 'brings us into some of the best company in the world'.[15] In 1905, the *Genealogist* also published an article about the life of Joinville's brother Geoffrey, who had settled in England and married the granddaughter and heiress of Walter de Lacy.[16] A further translation, this time by Sir Frank Marzials, the biographer of Charles Dickens and Victor Hugo, appeared in 1908, in the *Everyman Library*.[17]

The general reader could also read about Joinville and Saint Louis in a wide variety of other ways. In March 1866, they were both the subject of a reflective essay in the *Saturday Review* by the lawyer and essayist James Fitzjames Stephens and later included in his collection of essays *Horae Sabbaticae* published in 1892.[18] And in 1870, Max Müller, a Fellow of All Souls Oxford and member of the French Institute in London, published his own thoughts on the subject in a collection of essays (many published previously in journals) in his curiously named *Chips from a German Workshop*. Müller was prompted to put pen to paper by a review of Natalis de Wailly's *Histoire de Saint Louis* in the *Journal des Debats* and, after a discussion of the manuscript history and language of the text, encouraged his readers to read it themselves:

> Works like that of Joinville are most useful in dispelling that mist which the chroniclers of old and the romances of Walter Scott and others have

raised around the heroes of these holy wars. St Louis and his companions, as described by Joinville, not only in their glistening armour, but in their every-day attire, are brought nearer to us, become intelligible to us, and teach us lessons of humanity which we can learn from men only, and not from saints or heroes.[19]

Louis of course featured in histories of the crusades and chivalry[20] and he also inspired a number of biographies.[21] In 1855, the Revd John Hampden Gurney, vicar of Marylebone in London, published *St. Louis and Henry IV*, which was intended to educate and inspire young readers, and in 1870, on the 600th anniversary of Louis' death at Tunis, Anna Eliza Bray published *The Good St. Louis and His Times*. Both Gurney and Bray listed their sources, which included Joinville, Michaud, and English chroniclers such as Matthew Paris. Bray's history also included a brief survey of the crusading movement and she highlighted the crusading exploits of 'an Englishman' William Longsword, Earl of Salisbury, who perished at Mansurah. Others such as the Pirie Gordon family, lairds of Buthlaw in Aberdeenshire, laid claim to ancestors who had fought and died with Louis on crusade. In 1901, Edward Pirie-Gordon petitioned the pretender to the French throne for confirmation of the grant of a barony in the French peerage to his ancestor Sir William Gordon of Castle Gordon, co. Berwick, who had died with the king at Tunis.[22]

Further biographies appeared in the late nineteenth century, and the authors and series titles underline the way in which Louis's life had come to be portrayed as a Christian exemplar to follow.[23] In 1899, Duckworth published a translation of the biography of Saint Louis by Marius Sepet, in a series dedicated to 'Saints', with a Preface written by Revd George Tyrell, who described the subject as reaching 'the standard of heroic perfection as conceived in his day'.[24] And in 1901, Frederick Perry, a Fellow of All Souls and then a colonial administrator in South Africa, published *Saint Louis the Most Christian King* in the *Heroes of the Nations* series, which was intended to chronicle the lives of 'types of the several national ideals'.[25] Perry drew a clear parallel between the crusades and his own times:

> The crusades of Louis […] have been generally condemned in grounds of prudence and policy […] . But, if the motive may be regarded, he was induced by piety not ambition […] . If a single and disinterested aim, apart from the prospect of selfish advantage, can justify any war, his crusades were justified. And even on considerations of policy alone, it is not for an age which is beginning to chafe at Mohammedan dominion in western Asia to judge too harshly the last attempt which was made to overthrow it.[26]

This linkage between Louis's crusades and the perceived religious threat from Islam in the early twentieth century was highlighted again by Isabella Postgate writing in 1914 and, as will be discussed later, some contemporary poets. Postgate's history was entitled *Spirit of St Louis*, and for her the king was an example for evangelical Christians to follow in uncertain times. The Foreword was written by the Revd Charles Hart, and on her title page, she quoted the Dean of Durham, George Kitchin's own assessment of the French king: 'In Saint Louis chivalry received its crown; the fresh humanity of the time found its expression; religion was illustrated and ennobled.' Postgate concluded, 'the twentieth century is not an age of Crusades and pious pilgrimages; but there is even more need of Christian missionary zeal to stem the flowing tide of Islam all over the world.'[27]

Writing slightly later in 1917, Sir Henry Newbolt, a prominent writer and educationalist, published his *Book of the Happy Warrior* towards the end of the First World War, with the purpose of providing chivalric heroes for boys to emulate, with a chapter devoted to Saint Louis, drawing on the account provided by Joinville and focusing on his capture of Damietta, rather than his death at Tunis.[28]

Such works had a deliberate purpose to highlight the noble virtues and Christian sacrifice exemplified by Louis and even Charles Mackay, who included a lengthy chapter on the crusades in his *Memoirs of Extraordinary Popular Delusions*, commented that Saint Louis had left behind:

> one of the most singular reputations in history. He is the model king of ecclesiastical writers, in whose eyes his very defects become virtues, because they are manifested in furtherance of their cause. More unprejudiced historians, whilst they condemn his fanaticism, admit that he was endowed with many high and rare qualities; that he was in no one point behind his age and in many in advance of it.[29]

We also have a glimpse of how the life of Saint Louis was 'taught' in British public schools. At Rugby, William Charles Lake (later Dean of Durham) wrote of history lessons with Dr Thomas Arnold, in the 1830s: 'there were no characters which he taught us more to admire than some of the religious characters of the Middle Ages, such as Saint Louis of France and Pope Innocent III.'[30] And another pupil, Arthur Penrhyn Stanley, Arnold's biographer and later Dean of Westminster, commented: 'No expression of his reverence for a higher standard of Christian excellence could have been more striking than the almost involuntary expressions of admiration, which broke from him whenever mention was made of St. Louis of France.'[31]

In his poem dated 1867 and entitled *A Southern Night*, one of Arnold's sons, the poet Matthew Arnold, wrote of his brother William, who had died at age 31 on his way back from service in India:

> Some grey crusading knight austere,
> Who bore St Louis company,
> And came home hurt to death.[32]

Inspiring writers

Against this background, it is not surprising that Saint Louis inspired a number of other nineteenth-century poets and writers. In 1810, William Stewart Rose, a member of Parliament and friend of Scott and Byron,[33] published a short poem entitled 'The Crusade of St Lewis', while in 1873 Louis was chosen as the subject of the Newdigate Prize for poetry at the University of Oxford, which was won by Cecil Moore, who later became a clergyman in London. Moore praised the 'monarch-saint, the warrior of the cross' and drew an explicit link between Louis's example and contemporary missions in Africa:

> Now as then
> War with the infidel; the pagan mail
> Of secret debt, or open hate, shall fail
> Before the spirit's sword. Upon your brow
> Is stamped the silent witness of your vow.
> Not for the Holy Sepulchre contend,
> But for its holier occupant.[34]

Louis's crusades also inspired a long poem by Alfred Hayes, a Birmingham teacher, published in 1887, entitled 'The Last Crusade', beginning with the departure of the French fleet and ending with the arrival of the Lord Edward's expedition. The language is rather florid and dated but again it demonstrates the strong interest in and familiarity with the subject.[35] Several novels (for adults and children) were also set against the background of Louis's crusades, by authors as diverse as an Anglican divine, the companion of Princess Charlotte, and a fur trader in northwest America.[36]

The visual image

While portraits or drawings of Louis seem to be rare,[37] Louis's life inspired a number of artists, particularly those of the Arts and Crafts Movement. As a student at Oxford, one of its leading figures, William Morris, wrote a poem, 'Riding Together', set against the background of Louis's first crusade, which was published in the *Oxford and Cambridge Magazine* in 1856.[38] And an episode in Joinville in which a knight witnesses the death of a comrade is said to have inspired part of another of his works, *The Defence of Guinevere*.[39] The art critic and collector John Ruskin was also familiar with Joinville's history, having been introduced to it by the Bostonian art historian Charles Eliot Norton, and one of Norton's Lowell lectures in 1862–3 was on the subject of Saint Louis and chivalry.[40] In 1883, the London-based firm Silber and Fleming even included a small bronze statue of Saint Louis in its *Illustrated Catalogue of Furniture and Household Requisites*.[41]

It is therefore not surprising that Louis was featured in a number of stained glass windows by Morris and his circle.[42] In the chapel of Brighton College he is depicted standing, leaning on his sword, along with King Alfred and Joan of Arc, in a window in memory of the Revd Arthur Titherington, the College's headmaster from 1895 until 1906. In the parish church of Cheddleton in Staffordshire, he appears in another memorial window, together with Constantine, St Helena, and Charlemagne. He was also chosen one of 20 saints depicted in the east window at All Saints' Church in Cambridge and designed by another Morris associate, Ford Madox Brown.[43]

In these windows there is no explicit reference to his crusades but in the North aisle of Holy Trinity Church, Sloane Square in London, Louis is depicted in his royal robes with a roundel below showing a group of crusaders in action. The window, completed in 1910 and designed by Sir William Blake Richmond, depicted each of the virtues and the one associated with Louis was Hope.[44] At St Colmon Church, Colmonell in Ayrshire, a window commissioned by the lawyer and patron of the arts Robert Finnie McEwen in 1909 was designed by the artist Louis Davis and installed at the west end of the church the following year (Figure 6.1).[45] A short guide explained the symbolism of the design and the depiction of Louis as a Christian hero, accompanied by a Scottish crusader:

> On the next tier ride the Crusaders, led by Saint Louis, King of France, splendid in the full panoply of war. The trappings of his horse blaze with golden lilies – the famous emblem of his royal house. But the standard above his head displays the Rood 'in a glory' – the sign of [one] greater than the King of France. Following Saint Louis is Robert Bruce, Earl of Carrick, and those other gallant soldiers who burned with that noble rage to set up the Cross above the Crescent in the Holy City.[46]

The design for the St. Colmon window was displayed in an exhibition at Leighton House, Kensington in London, which means that this imagery would have been known to a much wider audience than just the parishioners of the recipient church.

Figure 6.1 St Louis in a window designed by Louis Davis; the window can be viewed in St Colmon Church of Scotland in Colmonell. Image courtesy of St Colmon Parish Church.

For those of French descent living in Britain and Ireland, Louis was also a natural choice for family memorials. Thus the Beaugois family in South Wales chose to have him depicted as a crusader for a memorial window for two members of the family, who had died in 1910 and 1911, in their local church, St Paul's in Barry, Vale of Glamorgan.[47] In Castletownshend in Ireland, Harry Clarke, a Dublin-based designer, was asked to feature Saint Louis in a window commemorating Colonel Kendall Coghill, a veteran of the Indian Mutiny who died in 1919. Coghill even claimed descent from the French king and himself fought in Egypt some 600 years later. One of the smaller lights also depicted Louis setting sail for the crusade.[48]

War memorials

Louis was similarly chosen for a number of war memorials. It is rarely possible to piece together the full story behind the commissioning of such memorials – why a particular subject was chosen, how the designer interpreted the commission, or the reaction of the grieving family and community – but the circumstances meant that they often turned to traditional imagery, drawing on their collective memory and heritage. The visual image can also often tell its own story.

The first such windows commemorated those who had died in South Africa in the Anglo-Boer Wars (1899–1902).[49] In the chapter house of Gloucester Cathedral Louis, described as a crusader and depicting valour in defeat, appears with Richard the Lionheart in a memorial to the 480 men of Gloucestershire who lost their lives. The window was designed by Christopher Whall, one of the most influential stained glass artists of the Arts and Crafts Movement.[50] In another Boer War window in Lichfield Cathedral, designed by John Lisle, who was the chief draughtsman of the firm of Charles Eamer Kempe, commemorating the dead of the South Staffordshire Regiment, Louis is described as 'a heroic soldier and sufferer in the crusades' and depicted kneeling before the crown of thorns. Installed in 1904, it was not a coincidence that this subject was selected in the year of the *Entente Cordiale*, which marked a significant improvement in diplomatic relations between England and France, and this shared history would later influence other war memorial windows.[51] Louis also appeared with other warrior saints and national figures at St Mary's Church, Nottingham, again in a design by Kempe.[52]

As a subject, he also very much appealed to those commissioning and designing memorials in the aftermath of the First World War, and not only for those who had lost their lives on French soil.[53] At St Matthew's Church, Pentrich in Derbyshire, Christopher Whall once again included Louis, along with Saints George and Michael, in a window in memory of Bernard Winthrop Smith, who fell at Ypres; Whall was also the designer of another 'Louis window' in the chapel of Gray's Inn in London.

At Darfield Church in Yorkshire, the rector and his wife commissioned a window from another firm of glaziers – James Powell and Sons – in memory of their son Lt Charles Sorby, who had died at age 20 from wounds during the second battle of Ypres in May 1915 (Figure 6.2). The window shows Saint Louis (robed as a king rather than a crusader), as patron saint of France, along with St George, the patron saint of England, and in his sermon at the service of dedication in June 1916, the Bishop of Sheffield praised the sacrifice of the young men of Britain.[54] And at St Catherine's Church in Canton, Cardiff, another stained glass designer (Daniells and Fricker) was commissioned to produce four windows commemorating parishioners who had died in various theatres of wars, including a window for Frederick Flook, who was killed at Paschendale in November 1917 and which depicted Saint Louis and St Joan of Arc.

This combination of French saints can also be found at Apethorpe in Northampton, along with St Leonard of Limoges, reflecting the dedication

Figure 6.2 Memorial window, All Saints, Darfield. Image courtesy of Rev. David Hildred.

of the church itself and commemorating Major Harold Brassey, who was killed in action in France in July 1916. And at Tenby in Wales, Kempe produced a five-light window in 'memory of all those who gave their lives for the cause of human right and justice in the Great War', which had the crucifixion at its centre with a selection of warrior saints, again including Louis. There are also other memorial windows which feature Saint Louis in St Peter ad Vincula, Chichester; Holy Sepulchre, Northampton; St Matthew and St Oswald's Church, New Bilton, Rugby; All Saints, Forton, Staffordshire; St Augustine's, Fenham, Newcastle; and St Julian's, Wellow, Somerset. These include Louis either as a symbol of France (in the case of Fenham also the Palestine campaign) or as one of a number of warrior saints and kings and commemorate either individual parishioners who had lost their lives in France or the fallen of the parish as a whole. In most, Louis is again depicted in his royal robes, but at the Church of the Holy Ascension at Oddington, Gloucestershire, there is a smaller image that appears to show him taking the cross, on his recovery from illness. And a figure of Saint Louis was also included in the Lancaster Gate Memorial Cross, designed by the architect Sir Walter Tapper. This originally stood outside Christchurch and commemorated the residents of the borough of Paddington who had died in the war. As Stefan Goebel has shown in his book *The Great War and Medieval Memory*, the choice of Louis was also not confined to churches of the Anglican community.[55]

Louis was also featured in some secular windows. At the great Gothic Revival house, Carlton Towers in Yorkshire, Lord Beaumont drew on aspects of British and family history for decoration, and a stained glass window in the East Hall featured Saint Louis, with St George and John the Baptist.[56] The geographical spread of such memorials and the number of different designers involved (as well as those who commissioned and paid for the memorials) underlines the way in which the story of Saint Louis, the Christian crusader king, had been adopted by Britain and Ireland.

What does all this signify? It shows that the life of Saint Louis and his participation in the crusades was a subject familiar to Victorian and First World War Britain, particularly through the lens of Joinville's history. Louis was seen (and taught) as a Christian exemplar for all ages, with parallels drawn with contemporaries preaching and defending the Christian faith against more modern adversaries. His life inspired British artists and writers. With the rise of the Arts and Crafts Movement looking back to the stories and events of the Middle Ages, Louis was chosen as a subject for memorials to those who had lost their lives in national wars, particularly in France, by a wide variety of designers and patrons throughout the British Isles. He can therefore justly be described as a warrior saint for Victorian and First World War Britain and Ireland.

Notes

1 Adam Knobler, 'St. Louis and French Political Culture', *Studies in Medievalism* 8 (1998), pp. 156–6.
2 Henry Hallam, *View of the State of Europe During the Middle Ages*, 4th edn. 2 vols. (London, 1826). Hallam (1, p. 40) described Louis as 'perhaps the most eminent pattern of unswerving probity and Christian strictness of conscience that ever held the sceptre in any country.'
3 For the historiography of the crusades, see Christopher Tyerman, *The Debate on the Crusades* (Manchester, 2011) and Elizabeth Siberry, 'The Crusades: Nineteenth-Century Readers' Perspectives' in *Engaging the Crusades, Vol. 1*, pp. 7–27.
4 See *Royal Collections Trust*, <www.rct.uk>, and *National Trust Collections*, <www.nationaltrustcollections.org.uk>, [both accessed 20 November 2019]. It was also in the library of Sir Walter Scott, <www.advocates.org.uk/library/catalogue>, [accessed 20 November 2019].
5 Mark Purcell, *The Country House Library* (New Haven, CT, 2017), pp. 198–9.
6 Mike Horswell, 'Creating Chivalrous Imperial Crusaders: The Crusades in Juvenile Literature from Scott to Newbolt, 1825–1917' in *Engaging the Crusades, Vol. 1*, pp. 31–3.

7 Susan Walton, 'Charlotte M. Yonge and the "Historic Harem" of Edward Augustus Freeman', *Journal of Victorian Culture* (2006), p. 230.
8 'Memoirs of John Lord of Joinville', *Edinburgh Review* (1809), pp. 469–77.
9 Review of Joinville in *Critical Review or Annals of Literature* 11 (1807), pp. 120–36 and *Monthly Review or Literary Journal* 55 (1808), pp. 67–80.
10 R.J. Moore-Collyer, 'Thomas Johnes of Hafod (1748–1816): Translator and Bibliophile', *Welsh History Review* 15 (1990–1), p. 410.
11 James Bohn, *Catalogue of Ancient and Modern Books in All Languages for Sale by James Bohn* (London, 1840); Siberry, 'Readers' Perspectives', p. 17
12 Publisher's note, Joinville, *Histoire de Saint Louis*, trans. James Hutton (London, 1868).
13 Quoted at ibid.
14 *Stories of the Olden Times from de Joinville and Froissart Arranged by M. Jones* (1870). My copy was awarded to 13-year-old Florence Buckland as a 'writing prize' in 1885.
15 Ethel Wedgwood, *The Memoirs of the Lord of Joinville* (London, 1906).
16 George W. Watson, 'The Families of Lacy, Geneva, Joinville and La Marche', *The Genealogist* n.s. 22 (1905), pp. 73–82.
17 *Memoirs of the Crusades by Villehardouin and De Joinville*, trans. F.T. Marzials (London, 1908).
18 Sir James Fitzjames Stephens, 'Joinville and St. Louis', *Horae Sabbaticae* (London, 1892), pp. 1–21.
19 F. Max Müller, *Chips from a German Workshop* 3 (London, 1870), pp. 159–200.
20 For example, Francis Warre Cornish, a master and subsequently Vice Provost of Eton from 1893 to 1916, wrote of him as an exemplar in his *Chivalry* (London, 1908), pp. 25, 128.
21 Travelers to Egypt were also very aware of Louis' crusade and captivity there. See, for example, Revd E.J. Davis, Chaplain of St Mark's Alexandria, *The Invasion of Egypt in AD 1249 by Louis IX of France and a History of the Contemporary Sultans of Egypt* (London, 1897).
22 East Sussex Record Office ASH/786. The outcome of the petition is not known.
23 Articles on Louis were also included in editions of the *Encyclopaedia Britannica*.
24 Marius Sepet, *Saint Louis* (London, 1899), p. x. A review in the *Spectator* (7 October 1899) compared Louis to other noble rulers such as King Alfred and Marcus Aurelius and commented, 'One cannot but read this work [...] without feeling the most profound respect and affection for this noble king, whose name is perpetuaed on the Mississippi, as well as in the hearts of all students of French history.'
25 Perry was one of a group of idealistic young men who worked for the High Commissioner Sir Alfred Milner. See Walter Nimocks, *Milner's Young Men* (London, 1970). Milner's aim was to build a structure 'capable of mounting a crusade for imperial unification', p. vii.
26 Frederick Perry, *Saint Louis* (London, 1901), p. 296.
27 Isa Postgate, *The Spirit of Saint Louis* (London, 1914), p. 50.
28 See Horswell, 'Imperial Crusaders', pp. 37–40. Winifred Knox, daughter of the Bishop of Manchester and sister of theologian Ronald Knox, also published *At the Court of a Saint* in 1909.
29 Charles Mackay, *Memoirs of Extraordinary Popular Delusions* (London, 1841), p. 457.
30 Trevor Park, *Nolo Episcopari* (St Bega, 2013), p. 57.

31 Arthur P. Stanley, *The Life and Correspondence of Thomas Arnold D.D.* (London, 1844), 1, p. 136.
32 This poem appeared later in a chapter on Saint Louis in Ethel Buxton's children's history of the crusades pubished in 1910.
33 Rose was suspected by Thomas Johnes of being the author of the hostile review in 1809 (see n. 8 above).
34 For missionaries and the crusades, see Horswell, *The Rise and Fall of British Crusader Medievalism, c. 1825–1945* (Abingdon, 2018), pp. 89–111.
35 Alfred Hayes, *The Last Crusade, and Other Poems* (London, 1887), pp. 1–131. The poetess Felicia Hemans, who was very popular in the early nineteenth century, apparently also planned to write a poem on the deathbed of Saint Louis at Tunis, as does one of the characters in Yonge's novel *Magnum Bonum* (1879). See Siberry, *New Crusaders*, pp. 131–3, 158–9.
36 Ellis Cornelia Knight, *Sir Guy de Lusignan* (1833); Alexander Ross, *Selma* (1839); John Mason Neale, *Stories of the Crusades* (1846); and Gertrude Hollis, *A Slave of the Saracens* (1907). See also Siberry, *The New Crusaders*, pp. 144, 157–8.
37 The exception seems to be book illustrations. For example, there is a sketch (in a private collection) attributed to Herbert Cole, a book illustrator much influenced by the Pre-Raphaelites.
38 William Morris, 'Riding Together', *Oxford and Cambridge Magazine* 5 (May 1856), pp. 320–1.
39 For a discussion of crusade references in Morris's work, see William Whitla, 'William Morris's "The Mosque Rising in the Place of the Temple of Solomon"; a Critical Text', *Pre-Raphaelite Studies* 9 (2000), pp. 43–81.
40 This laid the groundwork for his article 'Saint Louis and Joinville' in the *North American Review* 98 (April 1864), pp. 419–60.
41 These items were promoted as made 'to fit in alcoves or suitable for standing in halls.' *The Victorian Catalogue of Household Goods: A Complete Compendium of over Five Thousand Items to Furnish and Decorate the Victorian Home* (repr. London, 1991).
42 Peter Cormack, *Arts and Crafts Stained Glass* (New Haven, CT, 2015); A. Charles Sewter, *The Stained Glass of William Morris and His Circle* (New Haven, CT, 1975).
43 Ibid., pp. 33–4. Louis also featured with St Martin at St Alban's Church, Streatham Park.
44 Simon Reynolds, *William Blake Richmond* (Norwich, 1995), pp. 294–7.
45 Cormack, *Arts and Crafts,* pp. 170–84. The architect was Sir Robert Lorimer, who designed the 'Spirit of the Crusaders' war memorial in Paisley; Siberry, *New Crusaders,* pp. 99–100.
46 R.E.D. Sketchley, 'Benedicite Omnia Opera', Three Windows for Colmonell Church by Louis Davis (London, 1910).
47 Martin Crampin, *Stained Glass of Wales Catalogue*, <https://web.archive.org/web/20190702234849/http://stainedglass.llgc.org.uk/>, [accessed 25 February 2020].
48 Nicola Gordon Bowe, *The Life and Work of Harry Clarke* (Dublin, 1989), p. 120. Clarke also included Louis in a memorial window in Christchurch, Gorey, Co. Wexford.
49 Valerie B. Parkhouse, *Memorialising the Anglo-Boer War of 1899–1902* (London, 2015).

50 Cormack, *Arts and Crafts*, pp. 150–70 and *The Stained Glass Work of Christopher Whall* (Boston, 1999).
51 Adrian Barlow, *The Life and Legacy of Charles Eamer Kempe* (Cambridge, 2018), pp. 165–6.
52 Estelle Blyth, the daughter of the Bishop of Jerusalem, also included Louis in her children's book on *Warrior Saints* published in 1916, together with Saints Alban, Victor, Maurice, Sebastian, George, Martin, and Edmund and the secular heroes Alfred the Great, Godfrey of Bouillon, Joan of Arc, Sir Philip Sidney, and General Gordon.
53 See Siberry, 'Memorials to Crusaders: The Use of Crusade Imagery in British First World War Memorials' in *The Legacy of the Crusades: History and Memory*, eds. Torben Kjersgaard Nielsen and Kurt Villads Jensen, vol. 2 (Turnhout, forthcoming).
54 I am grateful to the vicar of Darfield for this information.
55 Stefan Goebel, *The Great War and Medieval Memory* (Cambridge, 2007).
56 The American stained-glass artist, Charles J. Connick, also included Louis, with Saints Maurice and George, in his war memorial window in the First Presbyterian Church in Greenbury, Pennsylvania. See Cormack, *Arts and Crafts*, p. 228.

Bibliography

Primary

Bohn, James. *Catalogue of Ancient and Modern Books in All Languages for Sale by James Bohn*. London: C. Richards, 1840.
Bray, Anna Eliza. *The Good Saint Louis and His Times*. London: Griffith and Farran, 1870.
Cornish, Francis Warre. *Chivalry*. London: Macmillan, 1908.
Crampin, Martin. *Stained Glass of Wales Catalogue*. https://web.archive.org/web/20190702234849/http://stainedglass.llgc.org.uk/. [Accessed 25 February 2020].
Gurney, John Hampden. *Saint Louis and Henry IV: Being a Second Series of Historical Sketches*. London: Longman, 1855.
Hallam, Henry. *View of the State of Europe During the Middle Ages*. 4th ed. 2 vols. London: John Murray, 1826.
Hayes, Alfred. *The Last Crusade, and Other Poems*. London: Simpkin, Marshall & Co., 1887.
Joinville, *Histoire de Saint Louis*. Translations:
    Hutton, James. London: Sampson, Low and Marston, 1868.
    Johnes, Thomas. Hafod: Hafod Press, 1807; and London: Bohn's Standard Library, 1848.
    Marzials, Frank. London: J.M. Dent, 1908.
    Wedgwood, Ethel. London: John Murray, 1906.
Knox, Winifred F. *Court of a Saint*. London: Methuen, 1909.
Mackay, Charles. *Memoirs of Extraordinary Popular Delusions*. London: R. Bentley, 1841.
'Memoirs of John Lord of Joinville'. *Edinburgh Review* (1809), pp. 469–77.
Morris, William. 'Riding Together'. *Oxford and Cambridge Magazine* 5 (May 1856), pp. 320–1.

Mûller, F. Max. *Chips from a German Workshop 3*. London: Longmans, Green, 1870, pp. 159–200.
Perry, Frederick. *Saint Louis the Most Christian King*. London: Putnam, 1901.
Postgate, Isabella Jane. *The Spirit of St. Louis: Stories of Chivalry and Sainthood*. London: Moring, 1914.
Sepet, Marius. *Saint Louis*. London: Duckworth, 1899.
Stanley, Arthur P. *The Life and Correspondence of Thomas Arnold*, D.D. London: B. Fellowes, 1844.
Stephens, James Fitzjames. 'Joinville and St. Louis'. In *Horae Sabbaticae*. London, 1892, pp. 1–21.
Stories of the Olden Times from de Joinville and Froissart Arranged by M. Jones. London: Cassell, Petter and Galpin, 1870.

Secondary

Barlow, Adrian. *The Life, Art and Legacy of Charles Eamer Kempe*. Cambridge: Lutterworth Press, 2018.
Bowe, Nicola Gordon. *The Life and Work of Harry Clarke*. Dublin: Irish Academic Press, 1989.
Cormack, Peter. *Arts and Crafts Stained Glass*. New Haven, CT: Yale University Press, 2015.
———. *The Stained Glass Work of Christopher Whall*. Boston, MA: Public Library, 1999.
Goebel, Stefan. *The Great War and Medieval Memory: War, Remembrance and Medievalism in Britain and Germany, 1914–40*. Cambridge: CUP, 2007.
Horswell, Mike. 'Creating Chivalrous Imperial Crusaders: The Crusades in Juvenile Literature from Scott to Newbolt, 1825–1917'. In *Perceptions of the Crusades from the Nineteenth to the Twenty-first Century: Engaging the Crusades, Volume One*. eds. Mike Horswell and Jonathan Phillips. Abingdon: Routledge, 2018, pp. 27–48.
———. *The Rise and Fall of British Crusader Medievalism, c. 1825–1945*. Abingdon: Routledge, 2018.
Knobler, Adam. 'St. Louis and French Political Culture'. In *Studies in Medievalism*. Vol. 8. ed. Leslie Workman. Woodbridge: Boydell and Brewer, 1998, pp. 156–76.
Moore-Collyer, R.J. 'Thomas Johnes of Hafod (1748–1816): Translator and Bibliophile'. *Welsh History Review* 15 (1990–91), pp. 399–416.
Nimocks, Walter. *Milner's Young Men: The 'Kindergarten' in Edwardian Imperial Affairs*. London: Hodder & Stoughton, 1970.
Park, Trevor. *'Nolo Episcopari': A Life of Charles John Vaughan, 1816–1897*. St Bees: St Bega Publications, 2013.
Parkhouse, Valerie B. *Memorializing the Anglo-Boer War of 1899–1902: Militarization of the Landscape, Monuments and Memorials in Britain*. London: Matador, 2015.
Purcell, Mark. *The Country House Library*. New Haven, CT: Yale University Press, 2017.

Reynolds, Simon. *William Blake Richmond: An Artist's Life, 1842–1921*. Norwich: Michael Russell, 1995.

Sewter, A. Charles. *Stained Glass of William Morris and His Circle*. New Haven, CT: Yale University Press, 1974.

Siberry, Elizabeth. 'The Crusades: Nineteenth-Century Readers' Perspectives'. In *Perceptions of the Crusades from the Nineteenth to the Twenty-first Century: Engaging the Cruasdes, Volume One*. eds. Mike Horswell and Jonathan Phillips. Abingdon: Routledge, 2018, pp. 7–27.

———. 'Memorials to Crusaders: The Use of Crusade Imagery in British First World War Memorials'. In *The Legacy of the Crusade: History and Memory*. eds. Torben Kjersgaard Nielsen and Kurt Villads Jensen. Vol. 2. Turnhout: Brepols, 2020.

———. *The New Crusaders: Images of the Crusades in the Nineteenth and Early Twentieth Centuries*. Aldershot: Ashgate, 2000.

Tyerman, Christopher. *The Debate on the Crusades*. Manchester: MUP, 2011.

Watson, George W. 'The Families of Lacy, Geneva, Joinville and La Marche'. *The Genealogist* 22 (1905), pp. 73–82.

Walton, Susan. 'Charlotte M. Yonge and the "Historic Harem" of Edward Augustus Freeman'. *Journal of Victorian Culture* 11 (2006), pp. 226–55.

Whitla, William. 'William Morris's "The Mosque Rising in the Place of the Temple of Solomon"; a Critical Text'. *Pre-Raphaelite Studies* 9 (2000), pp. 43–81.

7 The sultan, the Kaiser, the colonel, and the purloined wreath

Carole Hillenbrand

The sultan

When Saladin died on 27 Safar 589 (4 March 1193), it might have been expected that he would have asked his devoted courtiers to bury him in the Holy City of Jerusalem, which he had re-conquered for Islam in 1187. But this was not to be. Saladin's favourite place of residence was the city of Damascus where, far from the heavy demands of military campaigns, he rested each year enjoying the company of his family and his court. The great medieval Arab biographer Ibn Khallikan (d. 1282) wrote that Saladin 'liked that city and preferred it as a residence to all others'.[1]

His mausoleum (Figure 7.1) stands some 20 metres to the north-west of the much-venerated Umayyad mosque in Damascus. His body had been buried provisionally in the Damascus citadel on the day that he died. Ibn Khallikan wrote the following account of Saladin's burial: '[The body of] Salah al-Din remained interred within the citadel of Damascus until a tomb was built for its reception [...] to the north of the Great Mosque of Damascus.'[2] The medieval Arab historian Abu Shama (d. 1267) added further details. He described the building of the mausoleum and the removal there of Saladin's body by his eldest son, al-Afdal, who succeeded him as ruler of Damascus. According to Abu Shama, al-Afdal bought a house suitable for the burial place (of his father) to the north near the Friday mosque. He then ordered a *qubba* (domed shrine) to be built and he carried the body there on the Day of "Ashura in the year 592'.[3] The Day of 'Ashura, the tenth of the month of Muharram, is a sacred day for Muslims. The exact date on which Saladin's body, placed in a carved wooden sarcophagus, was taken from the citadel was Thursday 10 Muharram 592 (15 December 1195). It should be noted that Saladin's mausoleum is a simple square domed chamber of the type favoured for Ayyubid notables.[4] His coffin (Figures 7.2 and 7.3) is now covered in a cloth of green, the holy colour of Islam. There, in close proximity to the Umayyad mosque, the most prestigious sanctuary in Syria, this great hero rested in peace for some eight centuries.

The Kaiser's wreath 113

Figure 7.1 Exterior of Saladin's mausoleum, Damascus. Image by Jan Smith, <www.flickr.com/photos/26085795@N02/4708346719/>, CC BY 2.0, <commons.wikimedia.org/w/index.php?curid=14918984>.

The Kaiser

As John Röhl's biography points out, Kaiser Wilhelm II (1859–1940), was convinced that he 'had a duty to lead Germany to greatness'. Röhl describes the Kaiser as 'young, hot-headed Wilhelm II, eager for action and craving recognition'.[5] From 1890 onwards Kaiser Wilhelm set out to expand his empire eastwards, and indeed outside Europe, as a crucial element in his plan to make Germany a global power. The large-scale transportation of important monuments, or parts of monuments, from the Ottoman domains in Turkey, and from the lands that are now Jordan and Iraq, to be re-erected in the hugely expanded state museum in Berlin represented the cultural arm of this same policy. A high point of his increasingly provocative 'world power politics' (*Weltmachtpolitik*) was his spectacular state visit to Istanbul, Haifa, Jerusalem, Beirut, and Damascus in the autumn of 1898. Wearing the uniform of a Prussian field-marshal, he made a swaggering entry on horseback into Jerusalem on 29 October 1898 to consecrate the Church of the Redeemer, accompanied by the Empress Augusta. The impact of his visit

Figure 7.2 Saladin's coffins, Damascus. Image courtesy of the author.

to the city was considerable; indeed, a breach was made in the city wall to allow him to enter in style.

Moving on to Damascus, Kaiser Wilhelm visited the mausoleum in which, it was still generally believed, Saladin's sculpted walnut wood coffin had been finally placed on 15 December 1195.[6] There the Kaiser also saw a second coffin, lavishly made of white marble, which had been placed next to the wooden sarcophagus in 1878 by the Ottoman sultan 'Abd al-Hamid II; doubtless, to the sultan's mind, this was a more deserving sarcophagus for a personage as celebrated as Saladin than the twelfth-century masterpiece then in place. The great French historian of Islamic architecture, Jean Sauvaget, fiercely described this second coffin as 'horrible'. He explained that there were two coffins in the mausoleum which had been placed side by side; he much preferred the older one made from sculpted walnut, interlaced with geometrical designs and floral and vegetal decoration, which dates mostly from the Ayyubid period.[7] In his recent book on Saladin, Jonathan Phillips rightly points out that 'the cenotaph itself is of an Ottoman baroque style, a mark of modernity at the time, and it remains in place today, looking uncomfortably bulky next to its venerable stablemate'.[8]

Figure 7.3 Plaque on Saladin's coffin, Damascus. Image courtesy of the author.

During his visit to Saladin's tomb, the Kaiser praised Saladin as 'one of the most chivalrous rulers of all time', and referring to the Ottoman sultan, he declared: 'May the Sultan and the 300 million Mahomedans who live scattered throughout the world and who revere him as their Caliph, rest assured that the German Kaiser will be their friend for all time.'[9] The Empress Augusta then placed a bronze wreath on Saladin's tomb: this was a very dramatic gesture.[10] News of it spread across the Middle East and had a great impact. Indeed, as Huw Strachan points out, the rumours in the Arab street were that the Kaiser had even visited Mecca and converted to Islam; he was dubbed 'Hajji Wilhelm'.[11] And so, from 1878 until recently (see later), Saladin's mausoleum has housed two coffins, although there is no proof at all that Saladin's remains were ever removed from his simple coffin to the larger and grander newer one.

The colonel

Shortly before the Amir Faisal, who had led the Arab revolt against the Ottomans in 1916, made a theatrical entrance into Damascus on horseback on 1 October 1918, he had ordered some of his men to remove the Kaiser's bronze wreath from Saladin's tomb. Indeed, not surprisingly, the wreath had come to be viewed as a symbol of the Ottoman–German alliance hated by the Arabs. Amir Faisal stayed in Damascus only for a very short while. The British Colonel T.E. Lawrence, 'of Arabia', was with him at that time and, according to one account, it appears that Faisal presented him with the wreath. On 11 November that same year, the very day that the Great War ended, Lawrence gave the wreath to a museum in London, subsequently renamed the Imperial War Museum, and he claimed in his deposit note that he had removed the wreath himself: 'as Saladin no longer required it'.[12]

According to Lowell Thomas (d. 1981), Lawrence's devoted 'spin-doctor', Amir Faisal and Lawrence enjoyed a warm friendship. He wrote:

> Colonel Lawrence remained in Damascus only four days. But during that time he was the virtual ruler of the city, and one of his first moves was to visit the tomb of Saladin, where the Kaiser, back in 1898, had placed a satin flag and a bronze laurel wreath inscribed in Turkish and Arabic: 'From one great emperor to another.'[13]

It is interesting to note that Lowell Thomas misleads the reader by misquoting part of the inscription on the wreath.

The purloined wreath[14]

As the Imperial War Museum records on its website:

> The wreath is a very significant item accessioned as part of the IWM Collections. This significance relates not only to Lawrence, Feisal and the Kaiser, but also has a broader symbolic importance reflecting the German influence in the Ottoman empire, the end of the Palestine campaign and the portents for the post war political outcome for the region.[15]

The wreath is bronze with a gilt finish; at its widest it is 74 centimetres (Figures 7.4 and 7.5). When and where was it made? Kaiser Wilhelm probably ordered the making of the wreath some considerable time before he left on his famous journey to the Middle East. Such an elaborate artefact would have taken many weeks to create. It may be concluded that he had long intended to visit Saladin's mausoleum in Damascus and that he wanted to record that event with due pomp and ceremony. Where and when exactly the Arabic and Ottoman Turkish inscriptions were placed on the wreath is still unknown but it would seem most likely that this intricate work was carried out in Germany by an imported Ottoman calligrapher before the

Figure 7.4 The Kaiser's wreath, Imperial War Museum London, EPH 4338. Image courtesy of the author.

Kaiser left on his trip to the Middle East. It is time to look more closely at the detailed parts of this intricate artefact.

The crown

As with so much else in the royal progress of Kaiser Wilhelm through the Middle Eastern domains of the Ottoman Sultan 'Abd al-Hamid II, such as

Figure 7.5 The Kaiser's wreath, Imperial War Museum. Image courtesy of the author.

the gaudy, faux-Islamic triumphal arch hastily erected in Jerusalem to commemorate his visit, this wreath is packed with rather heavy-handed imperial symbolism. There is little doubt that its principal purpose is to exalt the Kaiser rather than Saladin, even though already at this stage this Kurdish hero was the most famous Muslim in the world apart from the Prophet Muhammad. And it exalted not just the Kaiser, but also his religion. For at the apex of his crown, and at the very top of the wreath, is a small cross; a much larger cross is at the centre of the crown's lower half, its importance underlined by the trefoil arch which outlines it and is much larger than the flanking arches which depict affronted eagles with outspread wings. This was the familiar way in which the German eagle (*der deutsche Adler*) was rendered in German imperial symbolism at the time (Figure 7.6).

The monogram and crown are superimposed on a semi-circular band draped over the top of the laurel wreath, a band which holds two eagles on either side of the crown. Between each pair of eagles there flaps the end of a fringed clerical stole bearing yet another cross in a medallion. Nor is this the last time the eagles appear: they recur in alternation with a cross in the semi-circular lower termination, like a swag, which reveals itself as the lower half of the curved band flanking the monogram. At the lower centre of this band there hangs a large Maltese cross with a tiny winged figure, legs akimbo, between each bar. So this tribute to Saladin comprises not a single Muslim element, neither crescent nor star, but instead has no fewer than *eight Christian crosses* and *ten German eagles*.

The crown is identical to that depicted in contemporary images of the Kaiser; it is in fact the imperial German crown. As for the laurel wreath as a signal mark of honour, this was eagerly adapted by German tradition from the classical Graeco-Roman past, and its individual overlapping crinkled leaves, berries, and twigs have been meticulously rendered.

The monogram reads W II IR, which can be translated as 'Wilhelm *der Zweite,* Imperator [et] Rex' and which was the way he signed himself.[16] The pomp and circumstance of this self-applied title of *IR* was gently mocked in later years as standing for '*Immer Reisend*' ('Forever on the Move') in reference to his love of travel. It thus has a peculiar and ironic relevance to this luxury object, connected as it is to one of his grandest tours. It is triumphantly of its time and place both in its tightly compressed design and

Figure 7.6 Imperial German eagle employed until 1918. David Liuzzo, *Wikimedia Commons.*

in the forms of the individual letters themselves. The crown clearly displays features which reflect the influence of German Art Nouveau (*Jugendstil*) which flourished in the 1890s and the early twentieth century.[17] The light serifs of the I and the II allude to the majesty of Roman lettering, but the bulging, spatulate letters, the powerful curves of the W, and the block-like power of the R have numerous *Jugendstil* parallels in contemporary German Gothic lettering of the more imaginative kind as found in books, posters, and coins.

The Arabic inscription under the Kaiser's monogram

The Arabic inscription placed under the Kaiser's monogram (Figure 7.7) is written in a finely controlled cursive calligraphic script. An attempt at translating it has been placed near the wreath in the Imperial War Museum. This anonymous translation covers only part of the whole inscription and, as it stands, it unfortunately contains a number of errors and omissions. It reads as follows: 'This crown was presented by His Majesty, the Emperor (His presence [*sic*], Wilhelm the Second in memory of his pilgrimage to the tomb of His presence [*sic*], Salah al-Din al-Ajubi [*sic*].' The Arabic term *hadratuhu*, mistranslated here as 'His presence', is a grandiose phrase meaning 'His Excellency'. The title written here as *al-Ajubi* refers to the family name of Saladin, Ayyubid, and it should be rendered as *al-Ayyubi*; Saladin's father was called Ayyub. Here is a full and accurate translation of this Arabic inscription: 'This crown was presented by the Lord of magnificence and grandeur, the Emperor of Germany, His Excellency Wilhelm II, as a memorial of the Emperor's visit to Damascus in order to eulogise His Excellency Salah al-Din al-Ayyubi, may the mercy of God be upon him, in the year 1315/1898.' The other inscriptions punctuating this circular wreath in six more or less equally spaced bands are in Ottoman Turkish. That is

Figure 7.7 Detail of Arabic inscription below the Kaiser's monogram, from Figure 7.4.

Figure 7.8 Detail of Arabic quotation at the bottom of the wreath, from Figure 7.4.

not an easy language at the best of times; and in this case the elaborate and rather mannered calligraphy creates further difficulties. But what it says, reading the six bands horizontally across the wreath from right to left in three successive tiers, is an Ottoman Turkish translation of the major Arabic inscription below the Kaiser's monogram, as presented earlier.

The Arabic quotation at the bottom of the wreath

The short Arabic quotation in flowing cursive script at the bottom of the wreath (Figure 7.8), 'Verily, God loves those who do good' – *inna Allaha yuhibbu al-muhsinin* – has resonances of Sura 12 of the Qur'an, entitled the Sura of Joseph. This chapter uses the term *al-muhsinin* ('those who do good') more often than any other chapter in the Qur'an. The story of Joseph and his brothers is told at considerable length in this chapter. In it, Joseph is presented as the epitome of virtue, who is merciful to his brothers despite their ill-treatment of him. It is no coincidence that here on the wreath placed on the tomb of Saladin there is an allusion to Joseph. One of Saladin's names, which is used frequently of him in the primary Arabic sources, is Joseph (his personal name in Arabic being Yusuf) and it is found repeatedly in the speeches and sermons that deal with his most famous triumphs – his victory at the Battle of Hattin and his re-conquest of Jerusalem. For example, the poet Ibn Sana' al-Mulk (d. 1211) praised Saladin after his glorious victory against the crusaders at Hattin in 1187 and he addresses Saladin with these words: 'You have never shown yourself in battles, without appearing, O Joseph, as beautiful as Joseph (in the Qur'an).'[18]

It should also be mentioned that the full title of the well-known biography of Saladin, written by his devoted administrator and friend Baha' al-Din Ibn Shaddad (d. 1234), is *Al-nawadir al-sultaniyya wa'l mahasin al-yusufiyya*

('The sultan's rare deeds and Joseph-like merits').[19] The semantic connection in Arabic between the word *mahasin* ('merits') and the Qur'anic word *muhsinin* ('those who do good') quoted on the wreath would not have been lost on any pious Muslim. This small inscription is therefore a well-chosen compliment to Saladin, extolling his rare accomplishments and achievements and his pious deeds which resemble those of his namesake, the Qur'anic Joseph.

Conclusion

Even without the presence of the wreath placed on Saladin's tomb by Kaiser Wilhelm in 1898, the story of Saladin's burial place in Damascus remains ongoing. Indeed, there has recently been an extraordinary and unexpected new chapter in the history of Saladin's burial place. It concerns a recently arrived third sarcophagus, which contains the body of Muhammad Sa'id Ramadani al-Bouti, a famous Syrian Sunni Muslim cleric and strong supporter of President Asad. Al-Bouti was assassinated in a mosque in Damascus in 2013.

Despite considerable local opposition, al-Bouti was not buried, as might have been expected, outside in the area adjacent to Saladin's tomb, an area which enshrines the graves of several senior Ottoman clerics and administrators and which is still within the compound of the shrine itself. Instead, the coffin of al-Bouti was placed inside Saladin's mausoleum, on the far left as one enters, and next to the large marble tomb donated by Sultan 'Abd al-Hamid II which has remained empty, despite his wish that Saladin's body should be placed within it.

Local people still firmly believe that Saladin's body has remained in the original wooden sarcophagus which is on the right when one enters the mausoleum. One might well ask why al-Bouti should have been put there and certainly this choice of burial place for him sparked controversy among Syrian opposition activists. Messages soon appeared on Twitter, apologising to Saladin and asking for his forgiveness. The funeral was televised live on 21 March 2013, showing crowds of men carrying a white-draped casket into the mausoleum. Perhaps these supporters felt it appropriate that al-Bouti should be placed in close proximity to Saladin, as al-Bouti was also a famous Kurd. The jury is still out on this issue.[20]

But to go back finally to the wreath, it may confidently be argued that its symbolism unmistakably vaunts the power of the Kaiser, whose monogram takes instant pride of place above the name of Saladin, who is effectively demoted twice, not only below the name of the Kaiser but also rendered on a much smaller scale. The symbolic meaning is clear: Saladin is less important than the Kaiser. In short it pretends to be one thing – a tribute to Saladin – but in reality it is quite another, namely a piece of imperial self-aggrandisement. Indeed, to many a Muslim eye its plethora of crosses, with their inbuilt crusading resonances, would seem a staggeringly insensitive way of honouring the very man who defeated the crusaders, captured Jerusalem and removed the giant cross from the top of the Dome of the Rock. In short, this whole wreath is an act of consummate colonialism – and all the more sinister if that motive was unconscious. No wonder Lawrence of Arabia, with his deep and passionate commitment to the Arab cause, loathed it and took it to London.

Acknowledgements

By writing this chapter I am discharging a debt of *pietas* owed to the late, much-loved and respected Jonathan Riley-Smith. I promised Jonathan that I would work on Saladin's wreath and I am happy to dedicate this contribution to his memory.

Notes

1 Ibn Khallikan, *Wafayat al-a'yan*, trans. Baron MacGuckin de Slane as *Ibn Khallikan's Biographical Dictionary*, vol. 4 (Beirut, 1970), p. 541.
2 Ibid., p. 546.
3 Abu Shama, *Kitab al-rawdatayn,* in *Recueil des Historiens des Croisades: Historiens Orientaux*, vol. 5 (Paris, 1906), p. 94.
4 The Ayyubids, in common with other Near Eastern dynasties such as the Zengids, the Rum Saljuqs and the Mamluks, followed a fashion widespread in the medieval Islamic world of building mausolea for their elites. For this process see O. Grabar, 'The Earliest Islamic Commemorative Structures. Notes and Documents', *Ars Orientalis* 6 (1966), pp. 7–45 and Thomas Leisten, *Architektur für Tote* (Berlin, 1998). As it happens, Ayyubid Syria was a particular hub for such buildings; the mausoleum of Saladin was a typical example.
5 John C.G. Röhl, *Kaiser Wilhelm II* (Cambridge, 2014), p. 73.
6 For an account of the building of the mausoleum of Saladin, see 'Abd al-Razzaq Moaz, 'Note sur le mausolée de Saladin à Damas', *Bulletin d'études orientales*, XXXIX–XL (1987–8), pp. 183–9.
7 Cf. Jean Sauvaget, 'Le Cénotaphe de Saladin', *Revue des Arts Asiatiques* 6 (1930), p. 168.
8 Phillips, *Saladin*, pp. 311–12.
9 Röhl, *Wilhelm*, p. 77. For more details on the history of this crucial period of German/Ottoman relations see, Volker Weiss, 'Der deutsche Dschihad', *Die Zeit,* 17 July 2014, <www.zeit.de/2014/30/erster-weltkrieg-dschihad-kaiserreich>, [accessed 24 February 2020].
10 Neil Faulkner, *Lawrence of Arabia's War* (London, 2016), p. 23.
11 Hew Strachan, *The First World War* (London, 2003), p. 98.
12 Imperial War Museum, Letter: EN1/1/TRO/002/2, <www.iwm.org.uk/collections/item/object/1020000758> and Wreath: EPH 4338, <www.iwm.org.uk/collections/item/object/30083872>, [both accessed 21 February 2020].
13 Lowell Thomas, *With Lawrence in Arabia* (New York: 1924), pp. 290–1.
14 Grateful thanks are due to the Imperial War Museum and especially Richard Bayford for a discussion about the wreath.

15 'Presentation Wreath from Saladin's Tomb', EPH 4338, IWM, <www.iwm.org.uk/collections/item/object/30083872>, [accessed 21 February 2020].
16 All translations unless otherwise indicated are the author's own.
17 For an overview of German Art Nouveau (*Jugendstil*), cf. Carol Belanger Grafton, *Art Nouveau* (Mineola, NY, 2018), pp. 53–82.
18 Jawdat Rikabi, *La poésie profane sous les Ayyoubides* (Paris, 1949), pp. 75–6; Carole Hillenbrand, *The Crusades* (Edinburgh, 1999), p. 179.
19 Baha' al-Din Ibn Shaddad, *Al-nawadir al-sultaniyya wa'l-mahasin al-yusufiyya*, trans. Donald S. Richards, as *The Rare and Excellent History of Saladin* (Aldershot, 2001).
20 Grateful thanks are due to Alasdair Gordon-Gibson for his pictures of Saladin's mausoleum and information about al-Bouti's tomb.

Bibliography

Abu Shama. 'Kitab al-rawdatayn'. In *Recueil des Historiens des Croisades: Historiens Orientaux* (Charles Adrien Barbier de Meynard, ed.). Vol. 5. Paris: Imprimerie nationale, 1906.

Faulkner, Neil. *Lawrence of Arabia's War: The Arabs, the British and the Remaking of the Middle East in WW1*. London: Yale University Press, 2016.

Grabar, O. 'The Earliest Islamic Commemorative Structures. Notes and Documents'. *Ars Orientalis* 6 (1966), pp. 7–45.

Grafton, Carol Belanger. *Art Nouveau: The Essential Reference*. Mineola, NY: Dover Publications, 2018.

Hillenbrand, Carole. *The Crusades: Islamic Perspectives*. Edinburgh: Edinburgh University Press, 1999.

Ibn Khallikan. *Wafayat al-a'yan*. Trans. William MacGuckin de Slane as *Ibn Khallikan's Biographical Dictionary*. Vol. 4. Beirut: Librairie du Liban, 1970 reprint.

Ibn Shaddad, Baha' al-Din. *Al-nawadir al-sultaniyya wa'l-mahasin al-yusufiyya*. Trans. Donald S. Richards, as *The Rare and Excellent History of Saladin*. Aldershot: Ashgate, 2001.

Leisten, Thomas. *Architektur für Tote: Bestattung in architektonischem Kontext in den Kernländern der islamischen Welt zwischen 3./9. und 6./12. Jahrhundert*. Berlin: Reimer, 1998.

Moaz, 'Abd al-Razzaq. 'Note sur le mausolée de Saladin à Damas'. *Bulletin d'études orientales* XXXIX-XL (1987–88), pp. 183–9.

Phillips, Jonathan. *The Life and Legend of the Sultan Saladin*. London: The Bodley Head, 2019.

Rikabi, Jawdat. *La poésie profane sous les Ayyoubides*. Paris: G.P. Maisonneuve, 1949.

Röhl, John C.G., *Kaiser Wilhelm II*. Cambridge: CUP, 2014.

Sauvaget, Jean. 'Le Cénotaphe de Saladin'. *Revue des Arts Asiatiques* 6 (1930), pp. 168–75.

Strachan, Huw. *The First World War*. London: OUP, 2003.

Thomas, Lowell. *With Lawrence in Arabia*. New York: Century Co., 1924.

Weiss, Volker. 'Der deutsche Dschihad'. *Die Zeit*, 17 July 2014. www.zeit.de/2014/30/erster-weltkrieg-dschihad-kaiserreich. [Accessed 24 February 2020].

Index

'Abd al-Hamid II, Ottoman Sultan 114, 117, 122
Abu Shama 112
Achilles 10
Acre 25, 60–1, 65–7, 76, 86
Adams, William 81
Aeneas 11
A History of the Crusades see Runciman, Steven
al-Adil 64
Aladdin (Disney) 30
al-Afdal, son of Saladin 112
al-Aqsa mosque 49
Albert of Aachen 9–10, 13, 15–16, 18–19
al-Bouti, Muhammad Sa'id Ramadani 122
Alexander of Macedon 75
Alexios I, Komnenos Byzantine Emperor 9, 13, 16
al-Fādil 45
Algeria 47, 66
Alice of Antioch 28, 34
Allenby, Edmund 78
Alfred the Great, King of Wessex 102
al-Qaeda 88
Alphonse of Toulouse 25, 36
Amalric, King of Jerusalem 32
Ambroise 60
Amer, Abdel Hakim 66
Andronikos Komnenos 62
Anna Komnene 13–16
Antioch 8, 14–17, 35, 42–4, 46, 66
Armstrong, Karen 49, 66
Arnold, Thomas 100–1
Arnulf of Chocques 13
Arslan 28, 33–4, 36
Arsuf, Battle of 79–80
Arthur (legendary king) 77
Asbridge, Tom 9, 11, 16–17
Assad, Bashar 122
Assad, Hafez 50
Assassin's Creed (video game) 61
Audita tremendi see Gregory VIII, Pope
Augusta Victoria of Schleswig-Holstein, German Empress 113, 115

Baldwin I of Boulogne, Count of Edessa, King of Jerusalem 8–9, 13
Baldwin II, Latin Emperor of Constantinople 95
Baldwin II, King of Jerusalem 30–1, 33
Baldwin III, King of Jerusalem 25–7, 31–6, 62
Baldwin IV, King of Jerusalem 43, 51, 67–8
Baldwin V, King of Jerusalem 62, 68
Balian of Ibelin (*Kingdom of Heaven*-character) 67–9
Berengaria of Navarre 64–5, 86
Berrini, Nino 63
Bertran de Born 60
bin Laden, Osama 50–1
Bloss, Celesta A. 25, 85, 89
Bohemund of Taranto 2, 8–9, 11–13, 16, 18
Bohn, James 97
Book of Martyrs see Foxe, John
Book of the Happy Warrior see Newbolt, Henry
Boy's Herald 81
Bramall, Richard 64

126 *Index*

Brassey, Harold 105
Bray, Anna Eliza 99
Britain 66, 95, 103–4, 106; British Isles 95; *see also* England, Wales
Brown, Ford Madox 102
Bruce, Robert, Earl of Carrick 102
Bush, George W. 50, 88
Butler, David 63, 67, 83, 87
Byron, George Gordon 101
Byzantine Empire 8–9, 13
Byzantium *see* Byzantine Empire

Cahen, Claude 9, 17
Cambridge 102
Cardiff 104
Cassell's Children's Book of Knowledge 81
Catlos, Brian 48
Chadwick, Elizabeth 29
Chahine, Youssef 49–50, 66, 76, 87–9; *El Naser Salah ad-Din* ('Saladin the Victorious') 50, 66–7, 76, 87
Chanson d'Antioche 10, 13, 17
Chanson de Jérusalem 10, 17
Charlemagne 3, 102
Charles Martel 75
Chichester 105
Chips from a German Workshop see Müller, Max
Christ *see* Jesus Christ
Coghill, Kendall 103
Cold War 63, 67–8
Conrad of Montferrat 4–5, 60–9, 84
Conrade of Montserrat *see* Conrad of Montferrat
Constance of Antioch 28, 34–5, 43, 47
Constantine the Great, Roman Emperor 102
Constantinople 63
Cooper, Abraham 80–2
Corrado, Marchese di Monferrato see Magnocavallo, Francesco Ottavio
Cottin, Sophie 78
Creswick, Paul 84
Critical Review 97
Crusader Kings (video game) 51
Crusades: First 4–5, 8–12, 15, 66; Second 25, 35, 43; Third 5, 45, 50, 60, 75–8, 83, 85–9
Csokas, Marton 68

Cyprus 43–4, 48
Cyrano de Bergerac 63

Damascus 5, 33, 43–4, 50, 112–16, 122
Damietta 100
David (biblical king) 52
Davis, Louis 102
Dayan, Moshe 49
De bello sacro see Herold, Johannes
Delingpole, James 52
DeMille, Cecil B. 62, 64–6, 86–7
Disraeli, Benjamin 11
Dome of the Rock 49, 123
Donachie, David 11, 16
Doré, Gustave 79–80
Douglas, David 7
du Garde Peach, Lawrence 61
Duggan, Alfred 12, 14, 16

Edessa 35, 43
Edinburgh Review 96
Edith (*The Talisman*-character) 63–4, 83, 85
Edward, Prince of England 96, 101
Egypt 43–4, 66, 95, 103
Eldridge, David 87–8
Eleanor of Aquitaine 25, 33, 85
Ellenblum, Ronnie 48–9
El Naser Salah ad-Din ('Saladin the Victorious') *see* Chahine, Youssef
Emma of Jericho 30
England 65, 78, 83, 96, 98, 104
Europe 8, 62, 65, 77, 86, 96, 113
Everyman Library 98
Ezechiel 46

Faisal I, King of Iraq 115–16
Felix Faber 26
First World War 5, 18, 87, 95, 100, 104–6, 116
Flook, Frederick 104
For Cross or Crescent see Stables, William Gordon
Foxe, John 47
France 5, 31, 34, 44, 50, 62, 66, 76, 95, 100, 102, 104–6
Frederick Barbarossa, Holy Roman Emperor 76–7
Fulcher of Chartres 15–16
Fulk V of Anjou 27–36

Gaspey, Thomas 81
Gay, Laverne 12, 16
Geoffrey II of Chalon 43
Geoffrey de Geneville 98
George, Saint 104, 106
Gerard of Ridefort 61
Germany 5, 113, 116
Gerusalemme liberata see Tasso,
 Torquato
Gesta Francorum 13, 15
Gibbon, Edward 7, 9, 77
Godfrey of Bouillon 5, 8–10, 16, 18
God's Wolf see Lee, Jeffrey
Goffredo (*Gerusalemme liberata*-
 character) 10, 14, 16
Grandi, Ascanio 11
Great War *see* First World War
Gregory VIII, Pope 45
Gregory, Philippa 20
Grousset, René 47–8
Guibert de Nogent 9
Gurney, John Hampden 99
Guy of Lusignan, King of Jerusalem
 28, 45–6, 60–1, 68–9

Hafod Press *see* Johnes, Thomas
Haifa 113
Hallam, Henry 96
Hamilton, Bernard 43, 45, 49
Hart, Charles 100
Hattin, Battle of 42–3, 45, 47, 61, 68,
 84, 121
Hayes, Alfred 101
Helena, Mother of Constantine the
 Great 102
Henry III, King of England 78
Henty, George Alfred 61, 86
Heroes of the Nations 99
Heroines of the Crusades see Bloss,
 Celesta A.
Herold, Johannes 46–7
Hewlett, Maurice 62, 65; *The Life
 and Death of Richard Yea-and-Nay*
 62, 64
Hijaz 42–3, 45, 49
Histoire des croisades (Michaud's
 history) *see* Michaud,
 Joseph François
Histoire de Saint Louis (Joinville's
 history) *see* Joinville, Jean de

Historia (Niketas Choniates' history)
 see Niketas Choniates
History of Chivalry and the Crusades
 (Stebbing's history) *see* Stebbing,
 Henry
History of England (Gaspey's history)
 see Gaspey, Thomas
History of the Crusades (Mills' history)
 see Mills, Charles
Hodierna of Jerusalem 30, 34
Holy City *see* Jerusalem
Holy Sepulchre 36, 101
Holy Warriors (play) *see* Eldridge, David
Horae Sabbaticae see Stephens,
 James Fitzjames
Hugh II, Count of Jaffa 28–34
Hughes, Maud 65
Hume, David 77
Humphrey IV of Toron 69
Husan al Din Lu III 4 I
Hutton, James 97–8

Ibn al Athir 44–5
Ibn Jubayr 44–5
Ibn Khallikan 112
Ibn Sana' al-Mulk 121
Ibn Shaddad 42, 44, 46, 77, 121–2
*Il Talismano; ossia, la Terza Crociata
 in Palestina* (Barbieri and Pacini) 63
Imad al-Din al Isfahani 77
Innocent III 100
Iraq 87, 113; US-led invasion of 49–50
Ireland 95, 103, 106
Iron Men and Saints see Lamb, Harold
Isabel, Queen of Jerusalem 60–2,
 67, 69
Istanbul 113; *see also* Constantinople
Italy 9, 11–12, 18, 61, 63
Itinerarium Regis Ricardi 44, 60
Ivanhoe see Scott, Walter

Jamila al-Jaza'iriyya (Jamila the
 Algerian) 66
Jane Eyre 61
Jerusalem 17, 19, 45, 75, 78, 85–8, 102,
 112–14, 118,; 1187 fall to Saladin
 of 45, 47, 50–1, 67–9, 77, 121, 123;
 Latin Kingdom of 17–18, 43–4,
 62, 65, 68, 87, 95; Melisende and
 26–36; Tancred and 7–8, 10, 13–16,

18; *see also* Amalric; Baldwin I of Boulogne; Baldwin II; Baldwin III; Baldwin IV; Baldwin V; Guy of Lusignan; Hodierna; Isabel; Maria Komnene; Melisende; Morphia of Melitene; Saladin; Sibyl; Tancred; Theodora Komnene
Jesus Christ 2, 14, 45, 75, 88, 95
Joachim, St 26
Joan of Arc 102, 104
Joanna of England, Queen of Sicily 64, 85
Johnes, Thomas 96–7
John, King of England 62, 65
John the Baptist 106
Joinville, Jean de 95–100, 102, 106; *Histoire de Saint Louis* 96, 98
Jordan 113
Joseph, biblical patriarch 121
Julius Caesar 75

Ka'aba 45
Kenneth (*The Talisman*-character) 62–4, 83
Kerak 49–50
Kingdom of Heaven see Scott, Ridley
Kings' Crusade (video game) 84
King Richard and the Crusaders (film) *see* Butler, David
Knight Crusader see Welch, Ronald
Knights of the Cross see Thomas, Edwin
Kugler, Bernhard 9, 17

Ladd, Alan 63, 67
Lake, William Charles 100
Lamb, Harold 64–5
Lampedusa, Giuseppe Tomasi di 11–12
La Princesse Lointaine see Rostand, Edmond
Lawrence, T.E. 5, 116, 123
Lee, Jeffrey 52; *see also God's Wolf*
Leonard of Limoges, Saint 104
Leopold V, Duke of Austria 61, 63
Le Pas Saladin 61
Lewis, Bernard 50
Libellus de expugnatione sanctae terrae 45
Liberata see Gerusalemme liberata

Lisle, John 104
London 97–9, 101–2, 104, 116–17, 123
Louis VII, King of France 43
Louis IX, St, King of France 5, 95–106
Loutherbourg, Philippe Jacques de 79, 81
Ludlow, Jack *see* Donachie, David
Luttrell Psalter 78

Mackay, Charles 100
Madden, Thomas F. 51
Magnocavallo, Francesco Ottavio 63
Maimbourg, Louis 78, 83
Mansurah, Battle of 95, 99
Manuel I Komnenos, Byzantine Emperor 43
Maria Komnene, Queen of Jerusalem 67
Mary, Mother of Jesus Christ 26
Marzials, Frank 98
Mathilde, Holy Roman Empress 11
Mathilde see Cottin, Sophie
Mayer, Hans Eberhard 25
McEwen, Robert Finnie 102
Mecca 43, 45, 48–9, 115
Medina 43, 45, 48
Meinhard II of Gorizia 61
Melisende, Queen of Jerusalem 4, 25–36
Memoirs of Extraordinary Popular Delusions see Mackay, Charles
Michael, Saint 104
Michaud, Joseph François 9, 17, 47, 79–80, 96, 99; *Histoire des croisades* 47, 79, 96
Milan 61, 63
Mills, Charles 60–1, 96
Monahan, William 67–8; *see also Kingdom of Heaven*
Montefiore, Simon Sebag 27
Monthly Review or Literary Journal 97
Moore, Cecil 101
Morphia of Melitene, Queen of Jerusalem 30, 35
Morris, Ernest 64
Morris, William 101–2
Mosse, Kate 26
Müller, Max 98
Muhammad 45, 118

Narratives of the Minstrel of Reims 61
Nasser, Gamal Abdel 50, 66, 87
Newbolt, Henry 100
Nicholson, Robert 9, 18
Niketas Choniates 60, 63
Norton, Charles Eliot 102
Nur ad-Din 43, 46

Onward P.C. Soldiers see Madden, Thomas F.
Oxford and Cambridge Magazine 102

Paris, Matthew 99
Pasha, Kamran 75, 88–9
Passio Reginaldi see Peter of Blois
Perry, Frederick 99
Peter of Blois 42–3, 46, 48, 52; *Passio Reginaldi* 42, 46, 48
Peter Tudebode 15
Philipp II, King of France 60, 62–3, 65, 67, 76–7
Pirie-Gordon, Edward 99
Porden, Eleanor 61
Postgate, Isabelle 100
Poussin, Nicolas 10
Prodomo, Alberto 26

Queen of Jerusalem see Mosse, Kate
Queen of Swords see Tarr, Judith

Ralph Niger 45
Ralph of Caen 9, 11, 13, 15
Rambaldo di Vaqueiras (I Monferrato) see Berrini, Nino
Raymond IV of St Gilles, Count of Toulouse, Raymond I of Tripoli 8, 25, 51
Raymond II of Tripoli 30
Raymond III of Tripoli 61
Raynald of Châtillon 4, 42–52, 62, 67–8, 84
Reynald, count of Sidon 64
Red Sea 43–5, 50
Reston, James 68
Ricchi, Pietro 10
Richard I, 'the Lionheart', King of England 5, 60–7, 75–89, 104
Richard I called Coeur de Lion at the Battle of Ascalon in the Act of

Unhorsing Saladin (painting) see Cooper, Abraham
Richard III (play by Shakespeare) 65
Richard and Saladin or The Crusaders of Jerusalem (spectacular) 82
Richard Coer de Lyon 61–2, 78
Richard en Palestine (Foucher and Adam) 63
Richard Ivinoe serdtse 64
Richard the Lionheart (TV-series) see Morris, Ernest
Richard the Lion-hearted (film) see Withey, Chester
Richmond, William Blake 102
Riding Together see Morris, William
Ridwan of Aleppo 8
Riley-Smith, Jonathan 51, 68, 123
Rinaldo (*Gerusalemme liberata*-character) 10, 13–14
Robert de Sablé 67
Robert the Monk 10
Robin Hood 86
Robson, William 96
Roger of Howden 60
Rose, William Stewart 101
Rossini, Gioachino 11
Rostand, Edmond 63
Runciman, Steven 9, 18, 27, 29–31, 36, 48–9, 60, 63, 66–8; *A History of the Crusades* 27, 48, 62
Ruskin, John 102
Rystar Kennet 64

Saint Louis see Louis IX, King of France
Saint Louis the Most Christian King see Perry, Frederick
Saladin 3–5, 42–7, 49–51, 60–8, 75–89, 112–23
Salah al-Din ibn Ayyub see Saladin
Saturday Review 98
Sayf al-Din 85
Schlumberger, Gustave 47
Scott, Ridley 4, 42–3, 50–1, 67–9, 86; *Kingdom of Heaven* 4, 42, 50–1, 67, 86
Scott, Walter 61–4, 66–9, 82, 84, 98, 101; *Ivanhoe* 61, 63, 66–7; *The Talisman* 61, 63–4, 66–7, 82–4, 86–7

Sepet, Marius 99
Shadow of the Swords see Pasha, Kamran
Sibyl, Queen of Jerusalem 28, 60, 67–9
Siege of Heaven see Thomas, Edwin
Sigebert of Gembloux, continuation of 25
Smith, Bernard Winthrop 104
Solomon (biblical king) 52
Sorby, Charles 104
Spirit of St Louis see Postgate, Isabelle
Stables, William Gordon 61
Stanley, Arthur Penrhyn 100
Stebbing, Henry 83, 85; *History of Chivalry and the Crusades* 84
Stephanie of Milly 67
Stephens, James Fitzjames 98
Stevenson, W.B. 47
St. Louis and Henry IV see Gurney, John Hampden
Stories of Olden Times see Hutton, James
Stronghold Crusader II (video game) 84
Stubbs, William 60, 68–9
Syria 49, 66, 112

Tancred 4, 7–19
Tancredi (*Gerusalemme liberata*-character) 10–11, 13–14
Tancredi (opera) 11
Tancredi (poem) 11
Tancredi Falconeri (*The Leopard*-character) 11–12
Tapper, Walter 105
Tarsus 9, 13
Tasso, Torquato 4, 8–10, 12–14, 16–18, 63, 67; *Gerusalemme liberata* 4, 8, 10, 13–14, 63
Tarr, Judith 4, 26–36
The Battle between Richard Coeur de Lion and Saladin in Palestine (painting) *see* Loutherbourg, Philippe Jacques de
The Black Knight 63, 68
The Crusade and Death of Richard I 61, 64
The Crusaders (opera by Benedict and Bunn) 63

The Crusades (1935 film) *see* DeMille, Cecil B.
The Flame of Islam see Lamb, Harold
The Genealogist 98
The Good St. Louis and His Times see Bray, Anna Eliza
The Knights of the Cross, or The Hermit's Prophecy (Beazley and Bishop) 63
The Last Crusade (poem) *see* Hayes, Alfred
The Leopard see Lampedusa, Giuseppe Tomasi di
The Life and Death of Richard Yea-and-Nay see Hewlett, Maurice
Theodora Angelina 62
Theodora Komnene, Queen of Jerusalem 62
The Prince and the Page see Yonge, Charlotte
The Talisman see Scott, Walter
The Talisman (1980–1 TV series) 64
The Wars of the Cross see Adams, William
Thomas, Edwin 12, 14, 16, 18–19
Thomas, Lowell 116
Tintoretto 10
Titherington, Arthur 102
Treasure magazine 82
Tunis 95, 99–100
Twist, John 63
Tyrell, George 99

United Arab Republic 66
United States 49, 51, 88
Usama Ibn Munqidh 15–16

View of the State of Europe During the Middle Ages see Hallam, Henry
Vivaldi, Vincenzo 10
Voltaire 10–11, 79

Wailly, Natalis de 98
Wales 103, 105
Walter I Grenier, Lord of Caesarea 30
Warriors of God see Reston, James
Wedgwood, Ethel 98
Welch, Ronald 66, 86
Whall, Christopher 104

Whitaker, David 64
Wilhelm II, German Emperor/Kaiser 5, 113–22
William V of Montferrat 61
William of Nangis 25
William of Tyre 10, 15–16, 25, 34, 36, 44, 47–8
Wine of Satan see Gay, Laverne

Winning His Spurs see Henty, George Alfred
Withey, Chester 63
With Richard the Fearless see Creswick, Paul

Yewdale, Ralph 9, 17
Yonge, Charlotte 96

For Product Safety Concerns and Information please contact our EU
representative GPSR@taylorandfrancis.com
Taylor & Francis Verlag GmbH, Kaufingerstraße 24, 80331 München, Germany